THE MYSTIC COOKBOOK

RECIPES, HISTORY, AND SEAFARING LORE

JEAN KERR

Globe Pequot

Guilford, Connecticut

Globe
Pequot

An imprint of The Rowman & Littlefield Publishing Company, Inc.
4501 Forbes Blvd., Ste. 200
Lanham, MD 20706
www.rowman.com

Distributed by NATIONAL BOOK NETWORK

British Library Cataloguing in Publication Information available

Library of Congress Cataloging-in-Publication Data available

ISBN 978-1-4930-3220-4 (paperback)
ISBN 978-1-4930-3223-5 (e-book)

∞™ The paper used in this publication meets the minimum requirements of American National Standard for Information Sciences—Permanence of Paper for Printed Library Materials, ANSI/NISO Z39.48-1992

Printed in the United States of America

CONTENTS

Acknowledgments   iv

Introduction   v

Fruit of the Sea   1

On the Half Shell: Bivalves   2

Oysters   2

Clams   14

Mussels   28

Scallops   34

Meet the Crustaceans   45

Crab   45

Lobster   53

Shrimp   64

Fin Fish   74

Bass   79

Cod   84

Flounder   94

Haddock   101

Halibut   107

Mackerel   112

Salmon   116

Shad and Shad Roe   124

Smelts   131

Squid   134

Swordfish   139

Tuna   145

Bounty of the Land   151

Fruit   152

Apples   152

Apple Cider   157

Blueberries   161

Cherries   165

Cranberries   168

Peaches   172

Strawberries   176

Vegetables and Legumes   178

Beans   180

Corn   184

Pumpkins and Squash   189

Pickles and Preserves   194

Fowl   197

Meat and Game   203

Breads and Baked Goods   209

Sweets   215

Photo Credits   222

Index   224

About the Author   233

ACKNOWLEDGMENTS

I am grateful to so many people for helping me expand the first edition of this book. While broadening the scope to include "land-based" recipes, I had the support and assistance of a number of award-winning chefs. I urge you to visit their establishments if you haven't already: Jasper White's famed Summer Shack restaurants (multiple locations in New England); Kerry Altiero's Café Miranda in Rockland, ME; Sam Hayward's Fore Street in Portland, ME; Daniel Bruce's family of restaurants at the Boston Harbor Hotel; Evan Mallet's Black Trumpet in Portsmouth, NH; and Joachim Sandbichler's Patio in Provincetown, MA. I also thank Jeff and Peaches Paige of Cotton in Manchester, NH and authors Judith Choate, Kate Krukowski Gooding, and Paulette Mitchell. There are a few chefs—Brandon Blethen, Leo Bushey, and Valerie Lareau—with whom I have since lost touch despite efforts to track them down. If you are reading this, please let's reconnect.

I am indebted to the Secret Agency, which made *Northeast FLAVOR* such a beautiful publication, and whose superb photography graces some of these pages. I also acknowledge my original co-author and publisher of *Northeast FLAVOR*.

I thank culinary experts and historians like Sandy Oliver, Paula Sullivan, and Ali Goodwin. Gratitude also to the farmers, growers, and producers like Clarkdale Farm in Deerfield, MA; Scott Farm in Dummerston, VT; Volante Farms; the King Arthur Flour Company; and Wyman's of Maine, who keep our New England traditions flourishing. Many thanks also to Mystic Seaport, a living embodiment of our New England heritage.

I am grateful to the Boleys, particularly my goddaughter, Nell, and her husband, Andy (and baby on the way). I will never forget that perfect fall afternoon of peaches and windfall apples and gleanings from the vegetable garden. I also thank our dear friend "Dudley" Durant, who showed us his secret cranberry bog and made wild cranberry muffins the next morning!

Thanks also to my extended family, the Helds, and Phyllis Held in particular, who is always an inspiration to me, in the kitchen and in life! I am also immensely grateful to my husband and my mum, who have both demonstrated endless patience and a keen eye for detail.

Many thanks to my editors at Globe Pequot, Amy Lyons and Katie O'Dell, and the great design and production team, who have made this new book such a feast for the eyes. And thanks to my original editor at Globe Pequot, Laura Strom, who is no longer with us, but believed in me and this project. Wish you were here.

INTRODUCTION

I have spent most of my life along the New England coast. My earliest summers were full of small adventures in rowboats and skiffs, which later became a bit bigger as I progressed to larger boats and sailing the Maine coast. We dug clams, picked mussels, caught flounder and striped bass. My family and friends would gather for big lobster dinners in the summertime. The kids would revel in sucking the meat out of the lobster legs until we grew big enough to warrant our own whole lobsters and graduated from hot dogs. In late summer, we walked just up the road for fresh-picked corn to accompany our feast, often with no more than twenty minutes between picking and eating.

We knew the fishermen and farmers nearby. We debated the relative merits of lobster claws versus tails, hard shell versus soft shell, and whether it was worth picking out the body meat. (My mother, who endured World War II rationing in Great Britain, was always picking apart the bodies long after everyone else had thrown in the napkin.) Anyone fortunate enough to grow up as I did will know that the New England experience and our history have a great deal to do with the ocean and the bounty that comes from it. The men and women who fished, tonged, dug, trawled, and trapped fish and shellfish did not have an easy life, but there was something that drew them to the sea, and they left a rich maritime history in their wake.

The first incarnation of this book was devoted exclusively to seafood history, stories, and recipes. Now, twelve years after writing *Mystic Seafood: Great Recipes, History, and Seafaring Lore from Mystic Seaport*, I have added another component. The perfect accompaniments to the bounty of our coastal waters come from the rich but stubborn land. I know well that locally grown corn is just as important to a New England summer supper as the juiciest lobster. This new edition presents recipes from the bounty of the land alongside the riches of the sea. While still exploring the history and culture of food in the Northeast, I have rounded up some of the most classic New England dishes. Some were born of necessity in days before our modern conveniences; others reflect an abundant harvest and celebrate seasonal gifts like strawberries in spring or cranberries in autumn. I have a deep appreciation not only for fundamental foods of the land like maple syrup, pumpkin, corn, venison, beans, and brown bread, but for the people of other cultures who arrived and made our culinary landscape more interesting and delicious.

As I rewrote this book, I became, once again, awed by the resourcefulness and ingenuity of those who lived in New England before the days of central heat, electricity, and various aids—like tractors and engines in fishing boats, weather forecasts, and GPS—that we now take for granted. And those who were here first, Native peoples and then early settlers, gave us the gift of finding varied and essential ways of preserving our food.

Beginning with the foods that were available before the first settlers arrived on these shores, through adaptations over time, to new twists on old recipes, we celebrate food: wild, cultivated, and created. There are recipes that date back to the earliest settlers (I don't think any of them go back further than salt cod, which was caught and preserved in vast quantities in the 1500s by Portuguese fishermen) up through the 1800s and beyond. Various chefs and food writers have put a delicious spin on the classics as well. The possibilities for fresh-picked strawberries are endless. The iconic cranberry, apple, and pumpkin nourish New England in their various seasons. New recipes here prove that they're not always just for dessert, either! Pickling and preserving recipes will give you the tools to savor local produce all year round and live the true northeastern wisdom: waste not, want not!

But to chronicle all these foods and recipes would be encyclopedic (and maybe a little boring). I just want you to cook, experiment, and maybe find a few interesting tidbits about our food history. Let this book inspire your next family meal. If you've always wondered what Blueberry Grunt was, perhaps the mouthwatering recipe will remind you to take advantage of the multitude of blueberry patches open for picking in the summer months. Traditional pies like Maple Walnut and Pumpkin are made even sweeter with local ingredients and the understanding of their New England roots. Round out a meal of Blackened Swordfish with New England Succotash, and get cozy in the wintertime with never-fail Baked Beans. I hope these stories and recipes deepen your connection to the bounty of New England, and enrich the meals you share. But most of all, I hope you enjoy this book, the recipes, and sitting down to a great meal.

FRUIT OF THE SEA

On the Half Shell: Bivalves

Oysters

"He had often eaten oysters, but had never had enough."

—W. S. Gilbert

My father died shortly before I began working on the first edition of this cookbook, some 12 years ago. I think he would have liked it, though food, with the exception of oysters, was not something of great interest to him. But every time I reread the tribute below, I remember my dad and smile. Then I go in search of a dozen or two on the half shell. After all, I come by it honestly.

In *The Art of Eating*, M. F. K. Fisher famously remarked: "There are three kinds of oyster eaters: those loose-minded sports who will eat anything, hot, cold, thin, thick, dead or alive, as long as it is an *oyster*; those who will eat them raw and only raw; and those who with equal severity will eat them cooked and no way other." My father counted himself among the first group—a man who never met an oyster he didn't like.

This was strange to me, as he was born in Lawrence, Massachusetts, in 1916, grew up in the dingy culinary tradition of a Scottish Presbyterian household, and otherwise could hardly be described as "a loose-minded sport." He liked hot dogs, beans, and brown bread; ham sandwiches, roast beef, and mashed potatoes. He had no love of swimming fish, but loved lobsters and shrimp. Watching him eat oysters was something altogether different, though, and a source of wonderful memories. When he ate oysters, a different side of him emerged. He approached oysters with a kind of reverence, savoring the complex briny tastes with great focus. It was a bit like watching someone listen to a favorite symphony. It was the only time I saw my father close his eyes when he ate.

For many years our Christmas dinners would begin with oysters on the half shell, an American tradition that originated in the late 1800s. My brother, the designated shucker, would have brought a peck of bluepoints up from Maryland that morning. After he arrived, presents were opened, then it was on to Bloody Marys and oysters. Then a standing rib roast of beef and plum pudding.

It was a dangerous thing to set the platter of freshly shucked oysters in front of my father—if you wanted any for yourself, that is. Eventually we all wised up and kept some back. Otherwise, by the time my diligent brother-shucker had removed his apron, I had mixed and delivered the Bloody Marys, and my mother had attempted unsuccessfully to fend my father off, the platter would hold perhaps one dozen, out or five or six dozen, for the three of us to share. I remember hearing him call out, "You'd better get in here if you want some of these!"

My father lived a long and happy life. Whether it had anything to do with the oysters, I can't say. I do know that he left us an oyster legacy. Not only do I still love oysters and still savor them as part of our family's traditions, but every time I taste the clear, briny ocean flavor of an oyster on the half shell, I'm offering a sort of tribute to my dad. I close my eyes and taste.

A Brief History of Oystering

Oystering certainly didn't start in the United States—people have been eating oysters since Roman times—but it has been an integral part of the American fishing scene from precolonial days.

Native Americans on both coasts ate oysters, as did the colonists, but it was in the nineteenth century that oystering really took off. Oysters were eaten in casseroles, stuffings, and stews. They were popular street food, grilled on braziers and eaten on the run—the nineteenth-century version of a slice of pizza to go. By the late 1800s, no elegant dinner was complete without a few dozen bluepoints to start.

To satisfy the American hunger for oysters, oystering became a full-fledged industry. Unlike most fishing, which didn't do much to maintain healthy stock levels, oyster fishermen seeded their own oyster beds, leaving some fallow to prevent overfishing and allow the oysters to grow to marketable size. Oysters grown in polluted waters such as New York Harbor were often moved to cleaner waters in Long Island Sound to purify themselves before they were sent to market. Oystering was almost certainly the first American aquaculture.

Oysters are harvested in shallow water. The traditional method uses tongs, scissor-like metal rakes that grab the oysters and pull them from the bottom. Oystermen stand in a boat's open cockpit and tong the oysters in water about 10 feet deep.

Dredging is another technique used for oystering. In the 1800s, flat-bottomed sailing vessels permitted oystering in shallow waters, while large sailing rigs made them

Dredges were towed along the bottom by sailing vessels such as the Mystic Seaport Museum's *Nellie*. Built in 1891, the *Nellie* was a sailing oyster dredger in southeastern Connecticut and Long Island's Great South Bay.

as fast as many yachts and minimized the time spent getting back and forth to the oyster beds.

Know Your Oysters

Although there are dozens of names for oysters in the United States, there are only four actual varieties. These four are, however, spread over such a wide range of coastline that they develop distinct local tastes and textures.

The eastern oyster is known by many names: the bluepoint (Long Island), Malpeque (Prince Edward Island), Chincoteague (Virginia), Breton Sound (Louisiana), Wellfleet (Massachusetts), and Cotuit (Nantucket), among others. Eastern oysters are eaten both cooked and raw. Those hailing from the colder waters in Canada and New England are usually firmer and somewhat brinier in taste. They are eaten year-round, although some folks feel that they are softer and less tangy in the summer months—the "non-R" months.

The belon or European oyster is raised both in the United States and throughout Europe. It is native to Brittany and eaten raw, not cooked. To many, it is the finest oyster for eating on the half shell. Belons, like Pacifics and Olympias, spawn during the summer months, which causes their taste and texture to be less appealing.

The Olympia oyster is native to Washington's Puget Sound but is found from Alaska to Mexico. It is small with a full, coppery taste and is eaten raw, not cooked.

The Pacific or Japanese oyster is the giant of the oyster family, sometimes reaching a foot in length. Although the larger specimens are too large for eating raw, the smaller ones are very good on the half shell. The flavor is sweet and mild. Because Pacifics grow so rapidly, they are cultivated throughout the world: on the West Coast of the United States as well as in Japan, Chile, and New Zealand.

Oddly, the tiny and delicate Kumamoto oyster is part of the Pacific family of much larger oysters. It is prized for its mild and creamy flavor on the half shell. Because it doesn't spawn in cold American waters, it is eaten year-round.

Are Oysters Really an Aphrodisiac?

Oysters as far back as classical Rome were thought to increase vitality, virility, and libido. Legend has it that Casanova used to put away fifty oysters just to start the day. While much of the aphrodisiac effect may be just a myth—or a placebo effect—scientists have linked the high zinc content and the presence of two rare amino acids in oysters to increased sexual desire. Whether fact or fiction, the oyster-as-aphrodisiac theory has been around for thousands of years and isn't likely to go away.

Oysters on the Half Shell

If you've never done it before, opening a raw oyster can be a real challenge. Frankly, it can be challenging even if you have. Not only is it difficult to see where you might insert a tool to pry the shell open, but the seal between the two shells is also very tight. Keep at it, and it'll get easier. It's a skill worth having.

You'll need an oyster knife, which has a long, flat blade with a rounded tip and a large handle.

The basic method is this: Find a sturdy glove or towel in which to hold the oyster. Place the oyster firmly on a flat surface with the flatter shell up and the hinged, narrow end toward you. Pushing firmly, wiggle an oyster knife into the hinge until the knife pushes past the hinge. Give the knife a quarter turn to break the seal. Run the knife against the top shell to disconnect it, and discard the top shell. Then run the knife under the oyster to disconnect it from the bottom shell so it will slide out easily—onto a fork or directly into your mouth. The liquid in the shell should be clear and briny, and the oyster should smell like the ocean.

Here are a couple of alternate techniques that, though frowned on by oyster pros, work fairly well:

- Use an old-fashioned V-shaped, hand-punch can opener to pry the oyster open at the hinge.

- Hang the wide end over the end of the counter and chip of a piece of shell with a hammer. Insert an oyster knife into the chip, and pry open by twisting the knife.

Serve oysters on a bed of shaved ice with lemon wedges and your favorite sauce; see the recipes for Mignonette Sauce, Cocktail Sauce, and "California Roll" Oysters that follow.

If this all seems like too much work, you can ask your fishmonger to shuck some oysters for you, but they should be eaten as soon as possible. An oyster on the half shell should be fresh, fresh, fresh.

Mignonette Sauce

This is a classic French sauce that seems to be preferred by oyster purists (although serious purists might stick to oyster with no sauce at all). It really does let the oyster flavor shine. Essentially, you are pickling minced shallots here, so make the sauce at least a couple of hours before you serve it. Invest in a good-quality vinegar—this will be smoother than a less-expensive one.

MAKES ABOUT ¾ CUP.

>   **2 tablespoons peppercorns—black or a mixture of pink, white, and black**
>   **2 shallots, minced**
>   **⅔ cup good, mild red wine vinegar or sherry vinegar**

1. Crush or grind the peppercorns and place them in a small jar.

2. Add the shallots and vinegar to the jar and shake well.

3. Chill for 2 hours or more.

4. Spoon onto raw oysters, to taste.

Cocktail Sauce

You can experiment with this recipe by using fresh herbs (I like dill and chives) and different kinds of hot sauces. One of my favorites is Tabasco brand Chipotle Pepper Sauce, which is milder and smokier than the company's regular hot sauce.

MAKES ABOUT 1 CUP.

>   **½ cup ketchup**
>   **⅓ cup prepared horseradish**
>   **2 tablespoons fresh lemon juice**
>   **Freshly ground pepper, sea salt, and hot sauce, to taste**

Mix all the ingredients in a small bowl and serve alongside raw oysters or any cold shellfish.

California Roll Oysters

This topping—an interesting departure from the usual oyster sauces—evokes the flavors of sushi-bar California rolls, with avocado, wasabi, and fish roe.

MAKES ENOUGH TO TOP A DOZEN OYSTERS ON THE HALF SHELL.

½ **avocado**

2 teaspoons prepared wasabi

2 teaspoons fresh lemon juice

Sea salt, to taste

Salmon roe or red lumpfish

1. Mash the avocado well in a bowl.

2. Add the wasabi and lemon juice and mix well. Salt to taste.

3. Top oysters on the half shell with this mixture—about ½ teaspoon each.

4. Sprinkle with salmon roe.

Bloody Mary

Oysters on the half shell seem to go beautifully with crisp white wines, such as Muscadets and dry Rieslings, but I love Bloody Marys with mine. Here's my recipe for this classic cocktail, which pairs well with just about any kind of seafood appetizer.

SERVES 1.

NOTE: YOU CAN MULTIPLY THIS RECIPE BY THE NUMBER OF GUESTS AND MAKE A PITCHER TO SAVE TIME.

4 ounces tomato juice

4 ounces Clamato juice

2 teaspoons Worcestershire sauce

1 teaspoon prepared horseradish

1 teaspoon fresh lemon juice

Dash of hot sauce

2 ounces vodka

Salt and pepper

Lime or lemon wedges, for serving

Celery stalk, for serving

Mix all the ingredients and pour into a tall glass over ice. Garnish with a wedge of lime or lemon (or both), and a celery stalk.

Fancy Roast Oysters

This is an adapted version of one of dozens of recipes for oysters from the 1896 *Boston Cooking School Cookbook.* By the time this cookbook was published, oysters were far more popular and presentable on the table than they had been a century and a half earlier, in colonial times. Like lobsters, as oysters became scarcer, they became more prized. In the 1787 *Compleat American Housewife,* oysters were mentioned only once; the *Boston Cooking School Cookbook* included nearly three dozen preparations.

SERVES 6 AS A FIRST COURSE.

> **3 tablespoons butter**
> **1 pint shucked oysters, drained**
> **Sliced brown bread**
> **⅓ cup chopped parsley**
> **Salt and pepper, to taste**

1. Melt the butter in a saucepan or frying pan.

2. Add the oysters and sauté them in the butter until they plump up and their edges begin to curl. Shake the pan gently to be sure the oysters cook evenly.

3. Serve the oysters on toasted brown bread cut into triangles and sprinkled with parsley. Season to taste with salt and pepper.

Oyster Stew

Boston's famed Union Oyster House serves this classic oyster stew.

SERVES 2.

> **1 pint light cream or half-and-half**
> **2 tablespoons butter**
> **16 raw oysters, freshly shucked, with their juices**
> **Paprika or finely chopped parsley**
> **Salt, pepper, Worcestershire sauce, and hot sauce, to taste**

1. Scald the cream or half-and-half by heating it until a thin skin forms on top.

2. Melt the butter in a small saucepan over low heat.

3. Add the oysters and their juices to the pan and sauté until plumped.

4. Combine the cream, butter, and oysters in a crock or soup bowl.

5. Sprinkle with paprika or parsley. Season to taste with salt, pepper, Worcestershire sauce, and hot sauce.

The Union Oyster House

The Union Oyster House at 41 Union Street in Boston is the oldest oyster bar in America—and the nation's oldest restaurant in continuous service as well. Its doors have been open since 1826, when the semicircular oyster bar was installed. It was here that Daniel Webster, a regular customer, drank a tall tumbler of brandy and water with his oysters, generally consuming at least six plates' worth. John F. Kennedy was a patron as well.

You can still get a stool at the bar and watch the expert shuckers opening oysters and clams and serving up their classic chowders and oyster stew. The oysters are shucked fresh as you watch, and you concoct your own cocktail sauce from jars of ketchup, horseradish, and hot sauce. It's a classic, and the model for many other venerable establishments across the country.

In 2003, the Union Oyster House was designated a National Historic Landmark.

Boston's Union Oyster House, founded in 1826 and still going strong. Photograph circa 1880.

Angels on Horseback

This is a recipe that has been around for ages, and most versions call for wrapping a shucked oyster in bacon and grilling it. I like the idea of broiling the oysters in their shells on top of the bacon and adding a pinch of Old Bay Seasoning.

SERVES 4 AS AN APPETIZER.

> **12 oysters in the shell**
> **3 slices thick-cut smoky bacon**
> **Pinch of Old Bay Seasoning**
> **Lemon slices, for serving**

1. Preheat the oven broiler.

2. Scrub the oyster shells thoroughly under cold running water with a wire brush.

3. Shuck the oysters, reserving each bottom shell. Place these shells in a baking pan on a bed of rock salt or crumpled foil to keep them flat.

4. Cut the bacon slices into 2-inch lengths or to fit a shell lengthwise. Place one piece in each shell. Broil until the bacon curls and renders its fat.

5. Place one oyster in each shell and turn to coat it with bacon fat. Broil until the oysters are just cooked through and curled at the edges, about a minute.

6. Remove the pan from the broiler and add a sprinkle of Old Bay Seasoning on each oyster. Serve with lemon slices.

Oysters Rockefeller

This is a classic and luxurious treatment of oysters. Countless chefs have introduced variations on the theme of spinach, bacon, and oysters; this is mine.

SERVES 4 AS AN APPETIZER.

2 slices thick-cut bacon

1 tablespoon butter

1 shallot, finely minced

6 cups loosely packed spinach leaves, chopped

1 tablespoon Pernod (optional)

¼ cup heavy or whipping cream

12 oysters on the half shell, drained

1½ tablespoons grated Parmesan cheese

1½ tablespoons bread crumbs

Fresh ground pepper, to taste

Lemon wedges, for serving

1. Preheat the oven broiler.

2. In a large, shallow pan, fry the bacon until just barely crisp. Drain on paper towels and set aside. Pour off all but a couple of teaspoons of the bacon fat. Add the butter to the pan.

3. Sauté the shallot in the fat until it's soft. Add the spinach and cook until just wilted.

4. Add the Pernod, if desired, and cream. Simmer for a minute.

5. Place a spoonful of the topping on each oyster. Top the spinach with a bit of crumbled bacon.

6. Mix the Parmesan and bread crumbs. Sprinkle equally over each oyster.

7. Broil until hot and bubbling. Grate some fresh ground pepper over each. Serve with lemon wedges.

Clams

"Your remark that clams will lie quiet if music be played to them, was superfluous—entirely superfluous."

—Mark Twain

In April 1884, the *Willimantic (Connecticut) Chronicle* reported that Mr. Orwell Atwood was moving for the summer season from his beautiful inland farm in Mansfield Centre to Stonington, near Mystic. The primary reason for the move, the *Chronicle* wrote, was that "the temptation following a favorable tide, to go a clamming . . . would be greater in that locality than at Mansfield Centre."

Many New Englanders can fully understand Mr. Atwood's dedication to clamming. In coastal New England, digging clams, eating clams, and having clambakes *is* summer. And it's been this way since the 1800s. But clams weren't always so popular.

Clams were one of America's original gathered foods. Though huge shell middens attest to the Native American taste for them in just about every coastal region of the country, it would be 200 years or more before clams would be fully appreciated by the non-Native population as the tasty morsels they are. The first settlers may have recognized

clams as a food that might keep hunger at bay; however, all too often European tastes and perceptions were negatively influenced by what the colonists perceived as "Indian food." Cotton Mather reported that during lean times, "the only food the poor had was acorns, ground-nuts, mussels and clams."

By the late 1800s, though, New Englanders had managed to romanticize the past and had created the popular myth that clambakes were a tradition of peaceable gatherings in which the Natives and settlers shared. There is no evidence that this is true, but clamming and clambakes had become extremely popular outdoor gatherings.

Taking a train to the seaside to a public clambake was a well-documented nineteenth-century pastime. In her wonderful book *Saltwater Foodways*, historian Sandy Oliver says, "Many large clambake pavilions were built after the middle of the century along the southern New England coast, especially near steamer or train terminals or trolley lines." She goes on to note that a "monster clambake" was held in 1864 near the mouth of Quiambaug Cove a little east of Mystic, Connecticut, and was attended by about 1,000 people.

Clams are harvested at low tide, usually on broad tidal beaches called flats. The traditional method is to dig for them using a clam fork—a sort of rake with four flat, foot-long tines, set at a sharp angle to a wooden handle. Veteran clam diggers usually have their favorite spots, often marked by numerous airholes in the sand. The tines are worked into the sand then the handle pulled back to reveal, one hopes, unbroken clams that can be pulled out of the sandy pile. These are placed in a clam hod—a wooden frame with a mesh or slatted basket allowing the clams to be easily rinsed in seawater.

Even after several rinses in the hod, however, it's a good idea to let the clams sit for a few hours in seawater (or a gallon of water with $^1/_2$ cup of sea salt dissolved in it). Some people add a cup of cornmeal to the water to help the clams rid themselves of sand and grit.

Clams are susceptible to "red tide"—a toxin that affects mussels, too. See the sidebar warning on the next page.

Size Matters

Although there are dozens of varieties of clams in the United States, East Coast clams fall into two major categories: hard shell and soft shell. Hard-shell clams come under the heading of quahog (pronounced *KO-hog*), which is a derivation of its Algonquian name. Clams in this category are classified by size. Littlenecks, named for Littleneck Bay in Long Island, are the smallest and considered by many to be the tastiest to eat raw on the half shell. Cherrystones, after Cherrystone Creek in Virginia, are midsize, and quahogs the largest. These are primarily used for sauces, chowders, and stuffings.

What's Red Tide—And Should I Be Worried?

The ocean is full of algae—microscopic plants that live and die unnoticed by humans. Given the right mixture of sun, temperature, and nutrients, however, algae can "bloom," rapidly multiplying. Most algae remain inoffensive, even when they bloom, but the *Alexandrium tamarense*, a one-celled phytoplankton, is the cause of red tide—and it's a real troublemaker.

Red tide doesn't bother fish, lobsters, or shrimp, but it does accumulate in filter feeders such as oysters, clams, and mussels. When these contaminated bivalves are eaten by humans, they can cause paralytic shellfish poisoning (PSP), resulting in severe illness and even death, although no deaths from red tide have been recorded in New England.

The effects of PSP come on quite rapidly after eating tainted shellfish and may resemble drunkenness. Get the infected person to a hospital without delay.

Fortunately, the coastal waters of the United States are constantly monitored for red tide by a network of government agencies and dedicated volunteers. When a red tide bloom is detected, shellfish beds are posted and closed, and sales are prohibited.

So if you're eating bivalves in a restaurant or buying them from a fishmonger, don't think twice about red tide. If you are collecting your own clams, oysters, or mussels, look for posted warnings and check your state government's website for red tide information.

Soft-shell or steamer clams are generally used for frying or eating steamed with butter. In addition to New England soft-shell clams, razor clams—named for their resemblance to an old-time straight razor—are excellent steamed, but are not nearly as common as plain old steamers.

Clambakes—A New England Tradition

We do our clambakes at the beach. A beach isn't a requirement, of course; a backyard is fine, but it will be a different experience. I think it's nice to have seawater available for cooking, washing, and swimming. If you're lucky enough to live near a public beach or have your own private beach, you can usually pull off a fine clambake with a little planning and a permit from the local fire department. Don't neglect the fire regulations—nothing ruins a good clambake like having the authorities show up and insist you douse the fire with everything half-cooked.

A clambake at Mystic, Connecticut, around 1900. Staples such as oysters and corn on the cob can be seen at the table on the right.

I always thought our clambakes were pretty unorthodox in that we steamed everything in a large metal trash can. (I am quick to point out to new guests that this is "the clambake can" and is not used for any other purpose.) It turns out that while the trash can thing is unusual, "cooking in the washtub" is pretty common—at least in Down East Maine—and a good deal simpler (and less sandy) than the traditional method of digging a pit, lining it with stones, building a large wood fire, burning the wood down to heat the stones, adding seaweed and food, and covering it all with a wet tarpaulin and steaming it for hours. That takes the best part of a day—my way takes only the best part of an afternoon. Should you wish to take the purist's route, however, there are excellent instructions in *The Joy of Cooking*.

Here's my method. We start out by scrubbing but not peeling Yukon Gold potatoes and wrapping each in foil. Allow one medium potato per person. Then we shuck the corn by pulling off the darker green leaves of the husk and pulling back but not detaching the softer inner leaves to reveal the corn silk. Pull the silk off and wrap the inner husk back around each ear. This protects the sweet kernels and makes a convenient handle when

Complete with brass band, this excursion by "an extra train" and steamer culminated at a big clambake at Rocky Point, Rhode Island.

pulled back after cooking. Corn shucking is a good task to delegate; with a cold beverage in hand, most people are happy to help.

Around this time we dig the fire pit. It's about 1 foot deep and 3 feet across. Lining the pit with a big flat rock keeps the moisture out and gives the pot something firm to sit on. Build a good hot wood fire in the pit, preferably using enough hardwood to keep the fire going for a couple of hours. It's got to be hot enough to boil seawater, which—because of its salt content—boils at a higher temperature than unsalted water.

Next, fill a big tub with ice, beer, maybe a few bottles of white wine, and anything else people might want to drink. Then head off to collect a bushel of rockweed from tide pools or rocky parts of the beach. You can distinguish rockweed by the little bubbles or "poppers" in the strands. Be sure not to confuse it with kelp, Irish moss, or other common sea flora that you find along the shore, which don't react well to heat. Rinse the rockweed in seawater and keep it handy. You'll need it as you cook. You'll also need sturdy pot holders and at least one strong helper.

Now you want to get about 8 to 10 inches of seawater in the bottom of the "kettle." Have the aforementioned helper help you lug the can down to the ocean. Try to wade out far enough to get clear, unsandy seawater. Lug it back, put it on the fire, and cover it till the water comes to a rolling boil.

Pile enough rockweed into the can to cover the bottom. Throw the foil-wrapped potatoes on top. Add more rockweed. Cover the can and let it steam/boil for about 20 minutes. You can throw in some whole onions at this point; they give a nice flavor to everything and taste great.

Next come the lobsters. We use pound to pound-and-a-quarter "bugs" because they are plentiful and cheap in the high season here in New England, and they fit nicely on a standard plate. Throw in the lobsters and cover with more rockweed. Replace the lid and steam for another 20 minutes or so.

Throw on the ears of corn in their green husks and cover with rockweed. Cook for 15 minutes. Add clams, preferably tied in individual cheesecloth bags for ease of removal, and again add rockweed. Steam just until the clams open, another 10 minutes or so. Throw out any broken or unopened clams. During this last step, we melt a pound of butter in an old enamel pot at the edge of the fire.

When everything is ready—and the timing here is more art than science—use tongs to decant everything into foil trays. You can also dump everything out onto a tarp, then have everyone grab a plate and dig in.

Our guests tend to eat on beach towels on the sand. Since the lobsters are often soft shells by mid- to late summer, they can usually be cracked by hand. Serve melted butter in disposable coffee cups for dipping clams and lobster and for dribbling on the corn and potatoes. Knives and forks are available but optional.

It will be obvious by this point that this is not a neat and tidy affair, nor is it low fat—unless you omit the butter, which is a mistake if you ask me. Nonetheless, I usually set out a bowl of lemon wedges.

In addition to the staples, I have been fortunate enough to have friends who bring all manner of wonderful things to accompany the feast, from sliced garden tomatoes to coleslaw, baguettes, and—last but not least—blueberry pie made from handpicked wild blueberries. It just doesn't get much better than this.

I happen to prefer the smallest hard-shell clams for eating raw, but other people swear by the slightly larger cherrystones. Whatever your preference, when served on the half shell, the flesh should be a pale rosy color and should smell fresh and briny. As with oysters, it takes some practice to become adept at opening clams.

The clammer in the foreground on a trade card for Doxsee's Pure Little Neck Clam Juice is using a rake with a single long handle, while his compatriot in the background uses a double-handled tong.

Clam digging can be hard on the back, but it's a New England tradition.

Rinse any sand or grit off the outside of the shell and allow the clams to rest for half an hour or so. If they are undisturbed, the shell seal may be a bit more relaxed. Hold a clam in one hand, preferably using a heavy glove, and work a clam knife in between the shells opposite the hinged end. Once the knife is between the shells, turn it to pry them open. Use the knife to detach the clam from the top and bottom shells. Discard one of the shells and place the clam in the other to serve. Like oysters, these can be served with Mignonette Sauce or a horseradish-and-ketchup-based Cocktail Sauce. (You'll find recipes for both in the "Oysters" chapter.) Serve with lemon wedges, allowing 6 clams per person as an hors d'oeuvre.

Basic Steamed Clams

Soft-shell New England clams are often called steamers and—unlike cherry-stones or littlenecks—are not eaten raw to the best of my knowledge. They are, however, delicious when cooked. To eat the steamed clams, pull the clam from the shell by the black "neck" or siphon. There is a covering over this that you will need to pull off with a thumb and forefinger. Then swish the clam around in the broth as a last-minute rinse, dip the clam in butter, and eat it whole. Mahogany clams, littlenecks, and cherrystones can also be steamed, but for my money, steamed clams are best with soft-shell clams.

SERVES 6 AS AN APPETIZER.

> **3 pounds soft-shell or steamer clams**
>
> **2 cups water, plus more as needed**
>
> **2 cups white wine or beer, plus more as needed**
>
> **Sea salt**
>
> **4 tablespoons melted butter**

1. Rinse the clams thoroughly to remove any grit or sand. Discard any that have broken shells.

2. Put the water and the wine or beer into a large, deep pot, adding more in equal parts until the liquid is 1 to 2 inches deep. Bring to a boil.

3. Add the steamers directly to the liquid or put them in a steamer basket. Steam over high heat until the clams open, about 5 minutes. Discard any that do not open. Strain the broth into a small bowl. Add the sea salt.

4. Serve, adding a small bowl of broth and a little melted butter on the side for each person.

Grilled Littleneck Clams with Garlic and Parsley

An Italian friend first served this wonderful dish to me. With people hanging around the grill, the clams never made it to the serving platter.

SERVES 4 AS AN APPETIZER.

    24 hard-shell littleneck or cherrystone clams
    3 tablespoons butter
    3 tablespoons extra-virgin olive oil
    1½ tablespoons finely chopped Italian parsley
    1½ tablespoons minced fresh garlic
    Lemon slices, for serving

1. Preheat a gas or charcoal grill. Rinse or scrub the clamshells until they're clean and free of sand and grit.

2. While the grill is heating, warm the butter and olive oil together in a small pan until butter is melted. Add the parsley and garlic, and sauté until the garlic is slightly translucent and fragrant, being careful not to brown it. Keep this mixture warm while you cook the clams.

3. Using a pair of tongs, place the clams on the grill and cook until they open. Using an oven mitt or heatproof glove, carefully twist the top shell off and place the full bottom shell back on the grill.

4. Spoon the garlic mixture over the clams and cook just until the mixture bubbles. Remove from the heat with tongs and serve with lemon slices.

Note: Depending on the size of the clams, the thickness of their shells, and the heat of the grill, they can take as long as 10 minutes to open but may begin to "pop" in as little as 2 minutes. Discard any that do not open.

Clams Casino

According to Linda Beaulieu, author of *The Providence and Rhode Island Cookbook*, Clams Casino originated with "Julius Keller, maitre d' in the original casino next to the seaside Towers in Narragansett." As with many classic dishes, there are numerous versions. This one uses quahogs, but you could use cherrystones if you prefer, doubling the number.

SERVES 6 AS A FIRST COURSE.

2 slices bacon

6 quahogs

½ cup water

1 tablespoon butter

3 tablespoons olive oil, divided

¾ cup finely chopped onion

4 cloves garlic

½ cup finely chopped green peppers

1 cup Italian-style dried bread crumbs

1 tablespoon chopped fresh oregano

½ teaspoon red pepper flakes

½ cup grated Parmesan cheese

2 tablespoons chopped flat-leaf parsley

Lemon wedges, for serving

1. Preheat the oven to 450°F.

2. In a large skillet, cook the bacon over medium heat until crisp. Remove the bacon from the pan, draining it on paper towels. Crumble into small pieces and reserve.

3. Wash the clams. Place them in a baking dish with the water. Bake until the clams open—about 15 minutes, depending on size. Discard any that do not open. When they're cool enough to handle, separate the shells and remove the meat, reserving the shells. Chop the clams coarsely and set aside. Reduce the oven heat to 400°F.

4. Add the butter and 2 tablespoons of the oil to the skillet, and sauté the onion, garlic, and peppers until soft.

5. Add the bread crumbs, reserved bacon, oregano, red pepper flakes, cheese, sautéed vegetables, and chopped clams. Mix well. Fill the clamshells with this mixture and place them on a baking sheet. Sprinkle with the parsley and drizzle with the remaining oil. Bake at 400°F for 10 minutes or until hot and beginning to brown. Serve with lemon wedges.

Spaghetti with White Clam Sauce

This Italian classic is a favorite in New England, too, especially in places like Boston's North End. It is simple to make but has a wonderful combination of flavors that really work well together.

SERVES 4.

> 4 dozen littleneck clams
> 3 tablespoons extra-virgin olive oil
> 3 tablespoons butter
> 4 cloves garlic, minced
> 2 tablespoons chopped flat-leaf parsley
> ½ cup dry white wine
> Salt and pepper

1. Rinse the clams well under cold running water. In a large stockpot, steam the clams in an inch of water until they open. When they're cool enough to handle, remove the meat from all but a dozen clams and chop coarsely. Strain the broth from the pan and reserve.

2. In a large skillet, heat the oil and add the butter. Cook over low heat until the butter is melted. Sauté the garlic until it's soft, about 3 minutes. Add the clam broth, parsley, and wine, and simmer for about 5 minutes. Add the clam meat and simmer for another 3 minutes.

3. Ladle over hot linguine or spaghetti and garnish each serving with 3 clams in the shell. Add salt and pepper to taste.

The Three Chowders

It's generally thought that the word *chowder* derives from the French word *chaudiere*, or "cauldron," referring to the pot in which coastal French fishermen made their fish soups. And though chowders may share this common ancestor, a debate has long raged in the northeastern United States about what constitutes a proper clam chowder.

Northern New Englanders swear by milk- or cream-based chowders, insisting that anything else is an impostor. The classic Manhattan Clam Chowder uses no dairy and is tomato based. What is known as Rhode Island Clam Chowder takes a middle ground by using neither dairy nor tomatoes, but simplifying matters to clams, broth, onions, and potatoes. And although I risk getting drummed out of my hometown in Maine by saying so, all three can be excellent.

Manhattan Clam Chowder

Long spurned by New Englanders, this tomato-based chowder was likely created by immigrants of Mediterranean descent. Garlic and herbs give it a distinct and delicious flavor, reminiscent of the classic seafood stew cioppino.

SERVES 8.

2 slices pancetta, diced

1 large onion, chopped

2 cloves garlic, minced

2 stalks celery, chopped

2 cups chopped (½-inch dice) peeled potatoes

½ cup chopped carrots

3 tablespoons flour

2 cups clam broth

2 cups Clamato juice

2 cups tomato juice

1 tablespoon chopped fresh oregano

1 bay leaf

2 cups chopped clams

1 tablespoon chopped Italian parsley

Olive oil, salt, black pepper, and hot sauce, to taste

1. In a large pot or Dutch oven, fry the pancetta until it's crisp and its fat is rendered. Remove from the pan, drain on paper towels, and crumble.

2. Add the onion, garlic, celery, potatoes, and carrots to the pot. Sauté for about 3 minutes.

3. Sprinkle the flour over the vegetables and add the broth, Clamato, and tomato juice. Bring to a boil, and continue boiling until the mixture begins to thicken.

4. Add the oregano and bay leaf, and simmer over low heat until the potatoes are soft, about 10 minutes.

5. Add the clams, parsley, and pancetta, and simmer for another 3 to 5 minutes. Drizzle with a little olive oil, season to taste with salt, pepper, and hot sauce, and serve with crusty bread.

New England Clam Chowder

This quintessential New England recipe has been around for many generations. In its original form, it often used condensed milk, as fresh dairy was often not available. This is a slightly updated version of the classic. I have made this using leftover steamer clams, but I prefer chopped hard-shell clams. This is best if made a day ahead.

MAKES 5 SERVINGS, 1 CUP EACH.

2 pounds cherrystone or littleneck clams

2 cups water

2 slices bacon, cut into 1-inch pieces

2 tablespoons butter, divided

1 cup chopped yellow onion

2 cups chopped (½-inch dice) potatoes

1 (12-ounce) can evaporated skim milk

1 cup half-and-half or light cream

2 teaspoons sea salt

1 teaspoon white pepper

½ teaspoon Worcestershire sauce

1. Rinse the clams thoroughly to remove any sand or grit from the outside. Bring the water to a boil and add the clams. Steam until they open, about 5 to 7 minutes. Drain the clams into a bowl through a strainer lined with several layers of cheesecloth or a coffee filter; reserve this broth. When the clams are cool enough to handle, remove them from their shells and chop coarsely. You should have at least ½ cup.

2. In a large pot, cook the bacon over medium heat until the fat is rendered and the bacon is crisp. Remove from the pot and drain on paper towels. Crumble or chop finely.

3. Melt 1 tablespoon of the butter in the pot and add the onion. Sauté for about 3 minutes until soft. Add the potatoes and stir to coat with melted butter. Cook for another 2 minutes over medium heat.

4. Add 1½ cups of the reserved clam broth and simmer until the potatoes are soft but not mushy, about 10 to 12 minutes. Add the clams and bacon and simmer for another 3 minutes.

5. Add the evaporated milk and half-and-half or light cream. Add the salt, pepper, and Worcestershire and stir to blend. Heat thoroughly, but do not boil. Float the remaining tablespoon of butter on top. Serve hot with crackers.

Flo's Rhode Island Clam Chowder

Just down the road from Mystic Seaport in Mystic, Connecticut, is a tiny breakfast-and-lunch restaurant by the name of Kitchen Little. It's well known for its Rhode Island Clam Chowder, a clear-broth chowder that leaves out the milk and cream. Being a New Englander, I was skeptical at first, but it is absolutely delicious—and less caloric than the standard New England Clam Chowder.

SERVES 6.

> 1 quart unopened quahogs
>
> 1 large onion, diced
>
> 6 tablespoons bacon grease
>
> 4 large red potatoes, diced
>
> ½ teaspoon white pepper
>
> 1 tablespoon chopped fresh basil

1. In a large pot or Dutch oven, bring an inch or two of water to a boil. Add the quahogs and steam until the clams have opened. When the clams are cool enough to handle, remove the meat and chop coarsely. Strain the broth from the pot and set aside.

2. Sauté the onion in the bacon grease until soft, about 3 minutes. Add the diced potatoes and clam broth to cover. If you need more broth, you can use bottled clam juice.

3. Bring to a boil and simmer over low heat until the potatoes are tender but not mushy, about 8 minutes. Add the clam meat and simmer for 2 minutes. Remove from the heat and stir in the pepper and basil. Serve hot with crackers.

Mussels

"The mussel pooled and heron priested shore. . ."

—Dylan Thomas

Until relatively recently, Americans have regarded mussels as the poor relations in the shellfish family. Although the colonists came from mussel-eating places in England and Europe, they didn't eat American mussels, possibly on the advice of Native Americans, who may have shunned them due to red tide risk. Not much had changed by the late nineteenth century, when Fannie Farmer described mussels as "an inferior sort of oyster" and didn't even provide a recipe for them in her 1896 *Boston Cooking-School Cook Book*.

In Europe, mussels have always gotten more respect. Blue mussels have been cultivated there since medieval times and have been a valued food source for many centuries. *Moules et frites* (mussels and french fries) is practically the national dish of Belgium, usually accompanied by a strong Belgian beer. In the 1970s, the French alone were consuming nearly thirty times more mussels than Americans. Now Americans are consuming ten times as many mussels as we did in the 1970s. We haven't caught up with the Europeans yet, but we're gaining.

How to Prepare Mussels for Cooking

The rope-grown farmed mussels available in the fish section of many supermarkets are wonderfully clean and often need less preparation than wild-gathered mussels, but you should still rinse and "debeard" them. The "beard" is the fibrous material that mussels use to attach themselves to the ropes, piers, rocks, or pilings on which they are growing. To remove it, feel the straighter side of the shell where the mussel is hinged. Grab any fibers between your thumb and forefinger and pull firmly. Use a small pair of pliers if you need to. Discard the beard and any mussels that gape open.

If you are using mussels you have gathered yourself, be prepared to rinse them thoroughly in several changes of seawater and, if possible, let them soak for a couple of hours to rid themselves of any grit. Scrub the shells with a stiff brush and scrape off any barnacles, then debeard as above.

In this country, mussels are cultivated on ropes and stakes. In New England, wild mussels are dragged or picked from the sea bottom. Some musseling operations drag up small seed mussels and replant them on leased beds until they reach marketable size. After the mussels are harvested, they are placed in saltwater tanks until they have purged themselves; then they're cleaned, graded, and sent to market.

The blue mussel is by far the most common in the United States, but the larger green mussel, usually imported from New Zealand, is gaining some in popularity.

It's easy to gather mussels yourself—easier than clamming or oystering—but there are a few things to keep in mind. Mussels should come from clean, open water at or below the low-tide mark, so you're going to have to get your feet wet. The mussels will be attached to rocks or pilings and will need to be well rinsed and scrubbed before you cook them.

In the waters around Mystic Seaport, for instance, there are hard clams (quahogs), scallops, and some mussels, but the shoreside development and the narrow inlets of the nearby harbors mean that much of the area is often closed to shellfishing.

Mussels Steamed in White Wine

This is similar to one of the simplest, most classic mussel preparations—the French *moules mariniere*—but uses garlic instead of shallots.

SERVES 4 AS AN APPETIZER.

> 1 cup dry white wine
>
> 3 cloves garlic, minced
>
> 1 tablespoon extra-virgin olive oil
>
> 4 dozen mussels, cleaned and debearded
>
> Lemon slices, for serving
>
> 1 small baguette, sliced, for soaking up cooking liquid

1. Combine the wine, garlic, and olive oil in a saucepan.

2. Bring to a low boil and add the mussels.

3. Turn the heat down so that the liquid is simmering, and cook until the mussels open wide enough to see the meat inside, 3 to 5 minutes. Discard any mussels that do not open.

4. Serve hot in bowls with lemon slices and sliced bread.

Sea Silk

The mussel's beard, the secreted fibers that it uses to attach itself to rocks, has long been woven into fabric. Ancient Greek fishermen used gloves woven of these fibers (called byssus) that were so durable, the gloves were handed down from generation to generation. Byssus cloth was being woven in Italy as late as the 1920s.

Mussels Fra Diavolo

This recipe is based on the classic Italian preparation. Once again, a loaf of good crusty bread is mandatory for sopping up the delicious pan juices. You could also serve this over linguine or spaghetti.

SERVES 4.

2½ tablespoons extra-virgin olive oil, divided

⅓ cup minced shallots

4 cloves garlic, minced

1 cup good-quality canned Italian plum tomatoes, coarsely chopped

2 tablespoons chopped fresh oregano

1 cup white vermouth

½ teaspoon hot red pepper flakes, or to taste

2 pounds mussels, cleaned and debearded

1. Heat 1½ tablespoons of the olive oil in a Dutch oven or large sauté pan. Add the shallots and sauté until soft.

2. Add the garlic, tomatoes, oregano, and vermouth, and simmer gently for 5 minutes. Add the red pepper flakes and stir.

3. Add the mussels and cover. Cook until the mussels are fully open, about 5 to 7 minutes. Discard any that do not open.

4. Drizzle the remaining tablespoon of olive oil over the mussels. Ladle the mussels into four small bowls, and ladle the remaining pan juices over them. Serve with warm crusty bread.

Spicy Thai Mussels

SERVES 4.

½ tablespoon butter

½ tablespoon olive oil

2–3 shallots, chopped

3 cloves garlic, peeled and sliced

1 (14-ounce) can whole tomatoes, juice reserved

1 stalk lemongrass, outside stalk removed, sliced lengthwise, then into 1-inch pieces

1 pint (2 cups) coconut milk

1 teaspoon chili garlic sauce (or more to taste)

1 cup white wine

1 cup clam juice

2 pounds mussels

2–3 scallions, split lengthwise, then cut into 2-inch pieces

1 tablespoon chopped cilantro

1. In a medium-size saucepan, heat the butter and olive oil over low heat. Sauté the shallots until translucent, about 3 minutes. Add 1 tablespoon of the garlic and sauté until soft.

2. Add the tomatoes to the pan, crushing them with the back of a wooden spoon. Add the lemongrass.

3. Add the coconut milk and chili garlic sauce, and let the mixture simmer over low heat until slightly thickened, 3 to 5 minutes. If the sauce seems too thick, add some of the canned tomato juice. You can prepare the recipe up to this stage and then refrigerate it for up to 2 days, if you like.

4. In a large pot, bring the wine, clam juice, and remaining garlic to a boil. Add the mussels and cook until they open.

5. Drain the mussels, discarding any that didn't open. Put them into a large, shallow serving bowl. Heat the cream sauce and stir in the scallions and cilantro. Pour over the mussels. Serve immediately.

Broiled Mussels with Parsley-Artichoke Pesto

This is a great appetizer for a dinner party when having everyone dive into a big bowl of mussels with their hands could get a little too messy. It would also make a great party hors d'oeuvre. Any leftover pesto can be frozen. You can also serve it over pasta, or spread it on French bread and broil until bubbling hot.

SERVES 4 AS AN APPETIZER.

> 1 cup chopped Italian parsley
>
> ¾ cup grated Parmesan cheese
>
> ⅓ cup mayonnaise
>
> 1 (14-ounce) can artichoke hearts, drained
>
> ⅓ cup olive oil
>
> Hot sauce, to taste
>
> ½ cup water
>
> ½ cup white wine
>
> 1½ pounds mussels, cleaned and debearded
>
> Lemon slices, for serving

1. Combine the parsley, Parmesan, mayonnaise, artichoke hearts, olive oil, and hot sauce in a food processor. Process until well combined.

2. Bring the water and wine to a boil in a medium saucepan. Add the mussels and steam, covered, until they open—3 to 5 minutes. Discard any unopened mussels.

3. Drain the mussels. When they're cool enough to handle, remove one shell and loosen the mussel meat from the other. Place the mussels in their shells on a baking sheet covered with crumpled aluminum foil to keep them level.

4. Spoon about a teaspoon of the pesto on top of each mussel, and broil until bubbling and hot, about a minute. Serve with lemon slices. Any leftover pesto or mussels would be great over pasta.

Scallops

"Sometimes, when I am out foraging the seashore at low tide, I become so interested in the pursuit of scallops that I forget to go in for my lunch, but I don't grow hungry. I just open a few scallops on the spot and eat their sweet muscles with no sauce but their own juicy, sea-given saltiness."

Euell Gibbons, *Stalking the Blue-Eyed Scallop*

When my husband and I got married way back when, we had invited, among other friends, a local fisherman known for his reticence as well as his fishing skills. He did not come to the wedding, but four months later, shortly before Christmas, he appeared on our doorstep with what was surely the most mouthwatering gift we received—a full 2 pounds of sea scallops, freshly caught just a few miles from our house, cleaned and delivered within hours of being on the seafloor. I'll take that over a candy dish any day.

Lobstermen in our part of New England have in previous years turned to scalloping during the winter months, when scallops are in season and lobsters aren't. There is no

expensive gear to be lost in winter storms, traps needn't be hauled and rebaited, and scallop prices are usually high enough to make it worthwhile. But it's hard work, nonetheless.

There are two primary types of scallops consumed in this country: bay scallops and sea scallops. Each type has its own following, but I prefer the larger and (generally paler) sea scallops. Since scallops are prone to drying out, the larger type allows more time for searing, browning, or frying without turning the scallops to rubber, which is easily done with overcooking. You can expect from 10 to 30 sea scallops per pound, and about 50 to 90 bay scallops.

Unlike most of the other bivalves we eat here in the United States, we consume only the large adductor muscle of the scallop, which is the muscle that opens and closes the shell. In Europe, scallops are cooked whole, including the roe, which turns a dull orange color when cooked. The adductor muscle is especially well developed in scallops as scallops can actually "swim." Unlike their stationary cousins, such as clams, mussels, and oysters, scallops can open and close their shells to propel themselves through the water. Some scallops wander farther afield than others, but all are capable of movement.

Scallops are either dredged from the ocean floor or caught by divers. "Diver" and "dayboat" scallops are more prized, as they tend to be treated more gently in the harvesting; they're also taken ashore—and thus to market—sooner. You may see scallops in the market that are labeled as "dry," and while intuitively this seems like a bad thing, "dry" scallops are preferable to scallops that have had moisture added to them to compensate for moisture loss after harvest. The dry scallops are more expensive per pound, but they are well worth the price. You know you are getting a fresher product, and you're not paying for the extra brine that has been added.

Until the early 1900s, scallops were not highly valued and seemed as much a source of culinary confusion as anything else. Even in France, where a greater variety of ingredients have been used for a longer time, it wasn't until the twentieth century that coquilles Saint-Jacques became popular. Even this is a bit confusing to Americans: In France, the term *coquilles Saint-Jacques* refers not only to the scallops themselves as an ingredient but also to a way of preparing them.

These days, scallops appear in dozens of preparations everywhere, from your local fish shack to Michelin-starred restaurants. Good scallops smell like fresh sea air, briny but slightly sweet, and have a taste that's almost as delicate.

Crispy Oven "Fried" Scallops

SERVES 4.

    2 eggs

    1 teaspoon fresh lemon juice

    20 large scallops

    Salt and pepper, to taste

    1 teaspoon paprika

    ½ cup all-purpose flour

    ½ cup butter, melted

    ½ cup bread crumbs, preferably Panko

1. Preheat oven to 475°F.

2. Whisk eggs and lemon juice thoroughly . Pat scallops dry with a clean kitchen or paper towel. Combine salt, pepper, paprika, and flour and mix well. Dip scallops in eggs and dredge in seasoned flour.

3. Dip scallops in melted butter and gently roll in bread crumbs. Place scallops on a wire rack over a baking sheet and drizzle with remaining butter. Bake for 5 to 7 minutes, turn carefully, and drizzle with any remaining butter. Bake for another 5 minutes, or until scallops are golden brown and cooked through. Serve with tartar sauce.

Broiled Scallops with Prosciutto

This is a favorite of mine—a take on the classic scallops-in-bacon hors d'oeuvre. It's delicious with a chilled Prosecco, an Italian sparkling wine.

SERVES 6 AS AN HORS D'OEUVRE.

    1 dozen sea scallops, halved
    ¼ cup horseradish (or your favorite) mustard
    ¼ pound prosciutto, cut into long strips
    1 lemon, cut into wedges, for serving

1. Preheat the broiler.

2. Spread a little of the mustard on each piece of prosciutto.

3. Wrap each scallop in a strip of prosciutto and secure with a small skewer or toothpick. Broil the scallops until just cooked through, about 3 to 5 minutes. Serve hot with lemon wedges.

Dave K's Scallop Casserole

Both of the lobstermen I know who scallop in winter prepare their scallops very simply in a way that lets the sweetness and freshness of the scallops really shine through.

SERVES 2–4.

> 1 pound sea scallops
>
> 3 tablespoons butter, divided
>
> 2 teaspoons fresh lemon juice, divided
>
> Salt and pepper, to taste
>
> 1 cup crushed Ritz (or similar) crackers

1. Preheat the oven to 450°F. Pat the scallops dry and cut them in half if they are very large.

2. Put half the butter in a casserole dish, and place it into the oven until the butter has melted. Remove the pan from the oven and add the scallops, half the lemon juice, and salt and pepper.

3. Melt the remaining butter in a small bowl or pan. Mix in the cracker crumbs and remaining lemon juice until well blended. Cover the scallops with this mixture. Bake for 15 to 20 minutes, or until the scallops are just cooked through and the topping is golden brown.

Escalloped Scallops

In *Old Boston Fare in Food and Pictures*, historian and chef Jerome Rubin chronicled the culinary life of Boston in a photographic history of New England's largest city and her people. The technique of "escalloping" is a classic preparation that usually involves cooking in a cream sauce and baking with a crumb topping. Following is an adaptation of Rubin's recipe for this traditional New England dish.

SERVES 4.

> 1½ pints (3 cups) scallops
>
> ½ cup white wine
>
> 1 pound mushrooms, sliced
>
> 1 green pepper, coarsely chopped
>
> 1 small onion, finely chopped
>
> 4 tablespoons butter, divided
>
> 2 tablespoons flour
>
> 1 cup cream or whole milk
>
> Buttered bread crumbs
>
> ¼ teaspoon paprika

1. Preheat the oven to 400°F.

2. Poach the scallops in the wine for 3 minutes and reserve the liquid (you'll need 3 cups). Drain, cool, and cut the scallops in half horizontally.

3. Sauté the mushrooms, green pepper, and onion in 2 tablespoons of the butter until soft.

4. Make a white sauce by melting the remaining butter in a saucepan. When it's melted, whisk in the flour and cook over low heat for 2 minutes. Gradually whisk in the cream or milk and the reserved scallop liquid.

5. Gently combine the scallops, vegetables, and sauce in a casserole dish. Top with the crumbs and paprika, and bake for 10 to 12 minutes, or until golden brown and bubbling.

Scallop Ceviche

I first had ceviche (pronounced *sah-VEE-chay*) in Key West, Florida, with a combination of seafood including conch. Scallops are naturally tender and become velvety soft and delicious when marinated in citrus.

SERVES 6 AS A FIRST COURSE.

½ cup lime juice

¼ cup blood orange juice

2 tablespoons Meyer lemon juice

¼ cup minced red bell pepper

1 poblano chile, minced (or jalapeño, if you like a little more heat)

1 shallot, minced

2 tablespoons chopped fresh cilantro

1 teaspoon grated fresh ginger

1 tablespoon sea salt

1 pound sea scallops, cut into half if large

Lime wedges, for serving

1. In a large glass or ceramic bowl, combine all the ingredients except the scallops and lime wedges. Add the scallops and toss well to coat.

2. Refrigerate for 4 hours or more, until the scallops are opaque and have absorbed the flavors of the marinade.

3. Serve cold in small bowls with a wedge of lime.

Nantucket Scallop Chowder

This dish is adapted from Imogene Walcott's recipe in her *Yankee Cookbook*, first published in 1939. She suggests removing the onions after they are sautéed, but leaving them in creates a more flavorful chowder.

SERVES 6.

4 tablespoons butter

2 small onions, sliced

1 cup peeled and diced potatoes

1 cup water

1 cup white wine or white vermouth

4 cups hot milk

1 pint (2 cups) scallops, cut into ½-inch pieces

Sea salt and white pepper, to taste

1. In a large saucepan, melt the butter over low heat. Sauté the onions until soft and golden.

2. Add the potatoes to the pan and sauté for 3 minutes.

3. Combine the water and wine or vermouth in a separate saucepan and heat till simmering. Add this mixture to the potatoes and simmer gently for 20 minutes.

4. Add the hot milk and scallops and simmer for another 5 minutes.

5. Season to taste with salt and white pepper. Serve hot with crackers.

Note: If you prefer a smoother bisque consistency, puree half the chowder in a food processor or blender and add back to the remaining chowder, mixing well.

Seared Scallops with Roasted Garlic and Yellow Pepper Sauce

This may seem like a lot of garlic, but when it's roasted, garlic has a sweet nutty flavor that enhances the natural sweetness of scallops.

SERVES 4.

1 head garlic

1 tablespoon olive oil

2 yellow bell peppers

1 shallot, minced

1 tablespoon fresh lemon juice

½ cup chicken or seafood stock

2 tablespoons butter

2 tablespoons flour

1 teaspoon salt

½ teaspoon white pepper

20 sea scallops

1. Preheat the oven to 350°F.

2. Peel the loose outer skin from the garlic, and cut off the pointed end of the head so the top of each clove is exposed. Drizzle with a teaspoon of the olive oil and wrap in foil, cut-end up. Bake the head until it's completely soft and golden and the cloves can be squeezed out, about 40 minutes. Squeeze the cloves into a bowl and set aside.

3. Broil the peppers whole, turning until each side is black and blistered. Remove from the heat and let cool, wrapped loosely in paper towels or a brown paper bag. When the peppers are cool enough to handle, peel off the blackened skin, remove the seeds and membranes inside, and chop coarsely.

4. Combine the roasted garlic, peppers, shallot, lemon juice, and stock in a food processor and blend until smooth.

5. Heat the butter and remaining olive oil in a frying pan over high heat. Mix the flour, salt, and pepper together in a shallow bowl. Roll the scallops in the flour mixture until they're lightly coated, shaking off any excess.

6. Sear the scallops in the frying pan until both top and bottom are nicely browned. Serve immediately over the sauce.

Seared Sea Scallops on Wilted Greens

This is a great preparation for winter when you are craving something light. You can often find good baby greens at winter farmer's markets.

SERVES 2.

¼ cup high-quality extra virgin olive oil

2 tablespoons fresh orange juice

1 tablespoon rice wine vinegar

Salt and pepper to taste

1 cup thinly sliced red onion

½ cup sundried tomatoes in oil, drained and thinly sliced

3 cups baby spinach or a mixture of kale, spinach, and other winter greens

6 large sea scallops

1 tablespoon safflower oil (or other mild oil)

½ tablespoon butter, melted

¼ cup crumbled goat cheese

1. In a large bowl, whisk together olive oil, orange juice, and rice wine vinegar. Season to taste with salt and pepper. Add onions, sun dried tomatoes, and spinach (or greens) and toss thoroughly until greens begin to wilt slightly.

2. Pat scallops dry and sprinkle tops and bottoms with salt and pepper.

3. Heat a heavy skillet, preferably cast iron. Add safflower oil and heat until nearly smoking. Add scallops and cook for 2 minutes. When scallops are nicely seared, turn and baste with melted butter in the pan. Cook for an additional 2 minutes.

4. Arrange salad mixture on plates, and place three scallops atop each. Sprinkle with goat cheese and serve.

Meet the Crustaceans

Crab

There are many species of crab worldwide. In northern New England, the most common are rock and Jonah crabs, which are surprisingly meaty, though the meat is somewhat difficult to extract. But the variety that constitutes most of the American crab fishery is the Atlantic blue crab, found roughly from Cape Cod down the eastern seaboard. The other important species from a culinary point of view are Florida's stone crabs, whose claws are particularly prized, the Pacific Dungeness crabs, and of course Alaskan king crabs. All are delicious, and the meat can be used interchangeably with the crabmeat specified in this chapter's recipes, though many would say that some of these delicacies are best enjoyed "neat" with perhaps some drawn butter.

About 50 percent of the eastern crab catch comes from the Chesapeake Bay, and that part of the country is justifiably famous for its crab cuisine. I have fond memories of a noisy, messy, and thoroughly enjoyable crab dinner in Maryland. The typical crab shack experience involves tables covered with newspaper, mallets for cracking the crab, spicy crab boil seasoning, and pitchers of ice-cold beer. It's not pretty, but boy, is it good.

"Picking" a crab is even more challenging than eating a lobster. The shells can be as hard or harder, and there is a smaller quantity of meat. Crab shacks often bring them a dozen to the order. Most of the meat is contained in the claws, though it's worth picking through to get the "lump" crabmeat from the body, as well as the "backfin" meat. Veteran crab pickers can pry and crack their way to about $2^{1}/_{4}$ ounces of meat per crab.

Although not as plentiful a fishery as it was twenty years ago, crabs are caught off the New England coast by lobstermen as a secondary catch. Often, for those anglers who had a patient wife at home willing to pick and pack the meat, it was supplemental income. More and more, our canned crab—like so many other products—is coming from Southeast Asia, where there are plentiful supplies of crab as well as cheap labor.

The only time when crabs are not so labor intensive is when they have molted and shed their hard shell. Before the new shell hardens again, they are sold and served as soft-shell crab. The first time you try one, it may seem odd to eat the crab claws, legs, and all, but they have incredible flavor and can be prepared quite simply. Blue crabs are the only crabs available in this form.

Basic Boiled or Steamed Blue Crabs

SERVES 2-4.

¼ cup vinegar

¼ cup seasoning, such as Old Bay

1 teaspoon salt

2 dozen lively blue crabs

1. Fill a large pot or Dutch oven with an inch or two of water. Add the vinegar, Old Bay or other seasoning, and salt.

2. Place a steaming rack in the bottom of the pot and bring the water to a boil.

3. Add the crabs, layering them in the pot, and steam for 30 minutes. Serve with butter, lots of napkins, and plenty of cold beer.

Make Your Own Crab Boil

Hard crabs are sold by the dozen or bushel, with a bushel of number ones containing 60 to 70 crabs. If you are planning a crab boil, allow about 6 crabs per person. As with lobsters, look for lively ones and use them as close to the time of purchase as possible. Discard any that seem limp or lifeless.

The Blue Crab Archives (blue-crab.org) offers this spice mixture recipe that you can make yourself and store in an airtight container. Add ½ cup or so when boiling or steaming crabs.

New Bay Seasoning

1 tablespoon sea salt

1 tablespoon celery salt

1 tablespoon ground dry mustard

1 tablespoon paprika

½ tablespoon mace

½ teaspoon cinnamon

½ teaspoon red pepper

½ teaspoon black pepper

½ teaspoon crushed red pepper flakes

¼ teaspoon ground cloves

Crab and Artichoke Dip

SERVES 6–8 AS AN HORS D'OEUVRE.

1 (14½-ounce) can artichoke hearts, quartered

½ cup mayonnaise

½ cup grated Parmesan cheese

1 clove garlic, crushed

1 shallot, chopped

¼ teaspoon hot sauce

Salt and pepper, to taste

1 cup crabmeat, canned, fresh, or frozen

1. In a food processor, blend all the ingredients except the crabmeat, until well blended but not smooth. Add the crabmeat and pulse until just blended.

2. Place the mixture in a ramekin or small casserole dish. Heat until bubbling and heated through. Serve with crackers or toasted pita chips.

Crab Louis

This is a classic but simple dish that makes a great appetizer or light lunch. Use the best crabmeat you can find. It's very similar to Creole Crab Remoulade.

SERVES 6.

1½ pounds lump crabmeat

1 cup mayonnaise

¼ cup heavy cream

¼ cup chili sauce

2 tablespoons chopped scallions

2 tablespoons finely chopped green pepper

1 tablespoon chopped pitted green olives

1 tablespoon fresh lemon juice

1. Divide the crabmeat among six chilled plates.

2. In a small bowl, combine the remaining ingredients and mix well.

3. Place a dollop of sauce on each plate and serve.

Crab Cakes

MAKES 8 CAKES.

¼ cup minced shallots

¼ cup minced green bell peppers

½ tablespoon olive oil

1 pound lump crabmeat, drained

12 saltine crackers, crushed

2 egg whites, lightly beaten

2 tablespoons mayonnaise

1 tablespoon fresh lemon juice

½ teaspoon Dijon mustard

Sea salt and white pepper, to taste

Dash of hot sauce

1½ tablespoons vegetable oil

1. In a small skillet, sauté the shallots and peppers in the olive oil until soft.

2. In a large bowl, combine all the remaining ingredients except the vegetable oil. Mix lightly with your hands until well combined. Divide into eight cakes.

3. Chill the cakes in the refrigerator for at least half an hour before cooking.

4. Heat the vegetable oil in a large skillet over high heat. Add the crab cakes and cook until golden brown on each side, about 4 minutes per side. Serve immediately with tartar sauce or cocktail sauce.

Crab Language

According to the Blue Crab Archives (blue-crab.org), male hard-shell crabs, preferred for their larger size and greater quantity of meat, are known as "jimmies." Adult female crabs are known as "sooks." They are graded numerically, with number one jimmies being the largest and meatiest crabs available. Number twos are usually smaller male crabs, and number threes are a mixture of ungraded smaller crabs, which may contain both males and females. "Busters" are crabs that are just about to shed their shell, while "peelers" are those that have just shed.

The Blue Crab Home Page (www.blue-crab.net) tells us, "The scientific name (*Callinectes sapidus* Rathbun) of the blue crab aptly describes the species. It was derived from Latin and Greek: *Calli*, beautiful; *nectes*, swimmer; and *sapidus*, savory. A literal translation might be the beautiful, savory swimmer. *Rathbun* refers to the late Dr. Mary Rathbun, who described the species in 1896."

Crab Cioppino

People have strong opinions about seafood stews such as cioppino and bouillabaisse, insisting that only a certain array of ingredients make them "authentic." My feeling is that most of these dishes originated with fishermen who were throwing whatever was left from their catch into their soup pots. We should feel free to do the same. Experiment with your favorite fish and shellfish.

If you can make the base (i.e., all but the fresh seafood) early in the day or even the night before, the flavors will have time to blend and develop and grow even more delicious.

SERVES 4–6.

¼ cup olive oil

1 large onion, peeled

1 tablespoon minced garlic

1 stalk celery, chopped fine

1 green pepper, coarsely chopped

¼ cup chopped Italian parsley

¼ cup chopped fresh oregano

1 (28-ounce) can whole Italian plum tomatoes

1 (6-ounce) can tomato paste

1 cup clam juice

1 cup water

2 cups dry red wine

18 littleneck clams

12 large shrimp, unpeeled

1 pound lump crabmeat

1. In a large pot or Dutch oven, heat the olive oil over medium heat. Add the onion, garlic, celery, and pepper, and sauté until soft. Add the parsley and oregano.

2. Add the tomatoes, tomato paste, clam juice, water, and wine to the vegetables and slowly bring to a boil. Simmer over low heat for 10 minutes.

3. Add the clams and simmer for 3 minutes. Then add the shrimp and crab and simmer for another 3 minutes, or until the shrimp are pink, the clams are open, and everything is heated through. Serve with warm, crusty bread.

Individual Maine Crabmeat Soufflés

This mouthwatering brunch dish originally came from the historic 1794 Watchtide by the Sea Bed and Breakfast, in Searsport, Maine. Sadly, this inn is no longer open, but this is a delicious memento.

SERVES 6.

2 tablespoons melted butter

½ pound Maine crabmeat

2 eggs

⅔ cup heavy cream

1 cup gruyère or Emmenthaler cheese

½ cup grated Parmesan cheese

Pinch of nutmeg

Pinch of thyme

Few grains of cayenne or hot sauce

Salt and pepper, to taste

1. Preheat the oven to 450°F.

2. Brush the insides of six ramekins with the melted butter. Divide the crabmeat among the ramekins, covering the bottom of each with crabmeat.

3. Separate the eggs and whisk the yolks together with the cream until light. Add any remaining butter and mix in the cheeses. Add the nutmeg, thyme, and cayenne or hot sauce, and season to taste with salt and pepper.

4. Whisk the egg whites to form stiff peaks; gently fold into yolk-cheese mixture. Gently spoon the soufflé mixture into the ramekins, filling each two-thirds full. Place the ramekins in a baking dish and add warm water to come halfway up their sides. Bake for 15 minutes, until the soufflés rise and their tops are puffed and golden brown. Serve immediately.

Pan-Fried Soft-Shell Crab

Soft-shell crabs are just hard-shell crabs after they've shed their shell and are harvested before the new one has hardened. It's a strange thing to eat the whole crab—I must admit I was skeptical the first time I tried it—but they are incredibly delicious and can be quite simple to prepare. Ask your fishmonger to "dress" them for you if possible. Otherwise a quick Internet search for "blue crabs" will yield a host of sites with instructions, recipes, and background.

SERVES 6 (2 CRABS EACH).

> 1 cup flour
>
> 1 teaspoon sea salt
>
> 1 teaspoon Old Bay Seasoning
>
> 12 soft-shell crabs, cleaned and dressed
>
> 1 cup vegetable oil, or enough to cover the bottom of a large skillet about ½ inch deep
>
> 3 tablespoons butter, melted
>
> Lemon wedges, for serving

1. Mix together the flour, salt, and seafood seasoning.

2. Dredge the crabs in the flour mixture to coat well. Shake off excess.

3. In a large frying pan or electric skillet, heat about ½ inch cooking oil to 375°F.

4. Add the crabs and reduce the heat to 350°F. Cook the crabs until browned, about 5 minutes on each side. Add the butter and flip crabs to coat. Serve hot with lemon wedges.

Lobster

"Although lobsters are highly unsightly, the sweet salty sensual delight of a claw dipped into drawn butter more than compensates for the lobster's cockroachlike appearance. . ."
—Linda Greenlaw, *The Lobster Chronicles*

Boiled lobster, broiled lobster, lobster bisque, lobster rolls—lobster in all its forms—may well be the most-prized delicacy to come from New England's chilly ocean waters. But this wasn't always the case. The history of lobster fishing is a rags-to-riches story.

If you were a young boy walking along the shore in a town like Mystic, Connecticut, in the 1700s, you might well find a 5- or even a 10-pound lobster just by looking among the rocks. You could feed a good-size family on just one of these giants, but you probably wouldn't even bother to pick it up unless your family was short of food or money. Prosperous people just didn't eat lobsters. Back then, lobsters were so plentiful that they were fed to prisoners and indentured servants in lieu of more valuable foods such as cod or mackerel. Small lobsters—those less than a couple of pounds—weren't considered worth the bother and were often dumped onto fields as fertilizer.

According to Colin Woodard in his book *The Lobster Coast*, coastal New Englanders had been catching and eating lobster since the 1600s, but no one had ever tried to establish a commercial, moneymaking enterprise from these crustaceans.

So how did lobster become such a prized commodity and such a culinary superstar? As always, the law of supply and demand can alter the course of just about anything. When lobsters were so abundant, they weren't worth much, but as they became recognized as a cheap and plentiful foodstuff, especially for feeding the increasing number of immigrant laborers that landed on the East Coast in the 1800s, a fishery grew up.

When the easy-to-catch tide pool lobsters became scarce, people started to fish from rowboats near the shore. But this couldn't meet the increasing demand from cities like New York. The sailing "lobster smack" was designed by New London fishermen to solve this logistical problem. Smacks had large tanks built into them. Salt water circulated freely through the tank, keeping a cargo of lobsters fresh for up to a week on their journey to the markets in New York City.

But it wasn't until the later 1800s that lobsters began to get some real respect. During Victorian times, New Englanders romanticized the lives of the earliest settlers, promoting the pleasant but fictional idea that our forefathers were taught how to create seaside feasts by local Native Americans. There's no evidence of this, although the coastal tribes were great shellfish eaters (as plentiful shell middens along the coast attest). Nonetheless, clambakes and shore picnics became hugely popular summer celebrations and included clams, chowder, lobster, potatoes, onions, breads, pies, and ripe watermelon— all the bounties of the season.

Lobsters became scarcer and more difficult to fish for as the demand increased. The rest, as they say, is history.

The familiarity that bred such contempt in colonial times is long gone, and the New England lobster industry is now highly regulated and very lucrative—if volatile. The investment required to enter the field is daunting. A far cry from gathering 5-pound lobsters in tide pools, fishermen or -women now must invest in a boat, gear, licensing fees, insurance, and dockage, as well as finding the best way to get their catch to market, often through a wholesaler or cooperative. The cost of entry to the fishery can run to $100,000 or more.

The size of lobsters that can be legally taken is strictly regulated. To be of legal size, a lobster's carapace or thorax must be at least $3\frac{1}{4}$ inches long. Female lobsters carrying fertilized eggs are also off-limits. You can tell a female lobster from a male by the tiny fins or "swimmerets" on the underside of the lobster-tail. The males have rigid ones, while the females' are flexible and fanlike.

When buying lobster, always look for lively specimens that wave their claws and snap their tails. These will keep in the refrigerator covered with a damp cloth or newspaper for 24 hours or so, but it's best to buy them as close to the time you're going to cook them as possible.

How to Eat a Lobster—and Maintain Your Dignity

No one was born knowing how to eat a lobster, although some crusty New England types might try to give you that impression.

There are two types of lobster eaters: those who pride themselves on getting every last little bit of edible meat out of the critter and those who confine themselves to the big parts and don't venture into those suspect areas with odd, unidentifiable bits.

No matter which kind of lobster eater you aspire to be, everyone begins the same way: with the claws and the tail. The claws are the easiest to get at. Take the lobster cracker (a seafood nutcracker, actually) and crack the claw through its thickest section. If you are unlucky, the claw will squirt precious lobster juice all over your shirt—or the plastic bib that the waitress has undoubtedly tried to tie around your neck.

Once you have the claw actually cracked, you can pull the meat out with the provided fork or lobster pick (which resembles an oversize dental instrument). Dunk it in melted butter and pop it into your mouth.

The knuckles between the claws and the body also contain tender and tasty morsels of meat. Crack them gently and push the meat out with a pick or finger.

Lobster Terms

Bugs: Slang term for lobsters, often used by fishermen.
Chicken lobsters or chix: Lobsters weighing between 1 and 1¼ pounds.
Cull: A lobster with only one claw.
Hard shell: Lobsters before the molt whose shells have hardened up. These have less liquid and more meat.
Jumbos: Lobsters weighing more than 2½ pounds.
Pound-and-a-quarters: Self-explanatory.
Selects: Lobsters from 1½ to 2½ pounds.
Shedders: Soft-shell lobsters that have just molted. These have more liquid and proportionately less meat, though the meat is often very tender.
Tomalley: The lobster's liver, considered by many to be a great delicacy.

Let's move on to the tail. Grasp the body in one hand and the tail in the other and twist as if you really mean it. The tail will come away from the body. At the juncture of the tail and the body is some stuff that I believe is best ignored; the good stuff is still inside the tail shell. At this point, more refined folks will take a knife, slit the underside of the tail lengthwise, and pull out the meat. The less refined will break off the end of the tail, stick their index finger in, and push the meat out. For obvious reasons, this is a technique more often seen at picnic tables than banquet tables. The tail meat is naturally divided lengthwise in half. I suggest you pull out the dark strip in the middle. (This is a harmless intestine of sorts, but we don't need to dwell on that.)

The little fins at the end of the tail in larger lobsters often have a bit of meat in them as well as some sweet juice. Break off the fins, place one between your teeth, and squeeze the meat out. This tooth-strainer method also works well for the four little legs on the each side of the body.

At the big end of the tail, you're going to find some unusual-looking "stuff" including the tomalley, which is the lobster's liver. Some love it; some caution that this is where any pollutants in the lobster would be concentrated.

Lobster Bytes
Courtesy of the Maine Lobster Promotion Council

- As a lobster grows, it sheds its shell, increasing in weight by 25 percent each time. A lobster will shed its shell twenty-four times the first year.
- A lobster is approximately seven years old before it is legal to harvest, and it will weigh about 1 pound.
- A lobster takes eighteen to twenty-four months to develop from time of impregnation to the hatching of the egg.
- An older lobster only molts every four or five years.
- A lobster is the size of a mosquito when it leaves the female's body.
- A lobster will catch fish, other crustaceans, and mollusks for its food.
- A lobster will commonly store food by burying it on the bottom of the ocean and defending the area much like a dog.
- A lobster's age is approximately its weight multiplied by four, plus three years.

The "red stuff" is unfertilized eggs called "coral"—probably only by the lobster marketing board. At one time they were considered a delicacy like caviar, but I think the only similarity is that they are both fishy eggs.

In the body cavity are some little bits of meat. It's easy to tell what's edible and what isn't. When in doubt, it probably isn't.

And if all else fails, just look for advice under your plate. Nearly every self-respecting lobster joint uses the same place mat: "How to Eat a Lobster."

Basic Boiled Lobster

Boiling a lobster is one of the easiest things you can do in the kitchen. All you have to do is watch your timer and make sure the lobsters are bright red when you remove them from the pot. If you are lucky enough to be near clean ocean water, by all means use it to boil your lobster.

SERVES 4.

> 6 quarts water
> ½ cup sea salt
> 4 (1¼- to 1½-pound) lively lobsters
> 1 lemon, cut into 4 wedges, for serving
> 6 tablespoons melted butter, for serving

1. Bring the water and salt to a boil in a pot large enough to also accommodate the lobsters with ease.

2. Plunge the lobsters into the boiling water headfirst and cover. Boil for 12 minutes.

3. Remove the lobsters from the pot and rinse them briefly in cool water.

4. Serve immediately with lemon wedges and/or melted butter.

Note: If you want to make it easier for your guests to remove the meat from the shell, you can split the tail lengthwise and crack the claws with a nutcracker or heavy knife. If the lobsters are soft shell, it's often possible just to crack the shells by hand.

To steam lobsters, bring 4 inches of salted water to a boil in the bottom of a large pot and add lobsters headfirst. Steam for 10-12 minutes or until bright red.

Lobster Rolls

There are many versions of lobster rolls and lobster salad throughout New England. This one is simple, and the taste of the lobster really shines through. If you want something a little fancier, you can serve it on a croissant or baguette, but grilled, buttered top-split hot dog rolls are classic.

SERVES 2.

2 lobsters (1 pound each), cooked and shelled; or ½ pound fresh lobster meat

2 tablespoons good mayonnaise

1 teaspoon minced celery

1 teaspoon minced onion

¼ teaspoon Old Bay Seasoning

2 split-top hot dog rolls

Butter

1. Mix the coarsely chopped lobster meat with the mayonnaise, celery, onion, and seasoning in a bowl. Refrigerate until you're ready to fill the rolls.

2. Butter the sides of the split-top hot dog rolls. Grill each side in a frying pan until just golden.

3. Fill the rolls and serve.

New England Lobster Casserole

This recipe is adapted from a Maine Lobster Promotion Council recipe (www .lobstersfrommaine.com). The council offers lots of information on lobsters, lobstering, and classic recipes as well as newer ones. In the late 1800s, when the lobster canning industry was in full swing, every frugal New England house-wife had a recipe for Lobster Casserole. At that time a can of lobster cost about 5 cents. Although canned lobster isn't available anymore, at least to my knowl-edge, this savory casserole is a wonderful—if less frugal—way to enjoy lobster, especially in the cooler months.

SERVES 4.

6 tablespoons butter, divided

1 pound cooked lobster meat, cut into bite-size pieces

3 tablespoons flour

¾ teaspoon dry mustard

1 cup milk

1 cup lobster stock or store-bought lobster base

Sea salt and fresh-ground pepper, to taste

8 ounces sliced mushrooms

1 garlic clove, finely chopped

1 tablespoon chopped fresh parsley

1 cup crumbled Pilot crackers or oyster crackers

1. Preheat the oven to 350°F.

2. In a saucepan, melt 3 tablespoons of the butter. Briefly sauté the lobster meat in the butter until it starts to turn pink. With a slotted spoon, remove the meat. Whisk the flour and dry mustard into the butter.

3. Stir in the milk and lobster stock, bring to a simmer, and cook until thickened, whisking constantly. Season to taste with sea salt and fresh pepper.

4. In a sauté pan, melt the remaining 3 tablespoons butter. Sauté the sliced mushrooms until they just start to give up their water. Remove the mushrooms from the pan. Stir the cooked lobster meat and sautéed mushrooms into the lobster sauce.

5. Add the minced garlic, chopped parsley, and cracker crumbs to the mushroom butter. Stir well to combine.

6. Grease a large casserole dish. Spoon the lobster-mushroom mixture into the bottom of the casserole. Cover with the buttered crumbs.

7. Bake until bubbly and the top is golden brown, about 20 to 30 minutes.

Lobster Croquettes

This recipe comes from the *Rumford Complete Cookbook* by Lily Haxworth Wallace, a "lecturer, teacher and writer on domestic science." The book was first published by the Rumford Company in Providence, Rhode Island, in 1908. These would make an excellent hors d'oeuvre or brunch dish with eggs.

SERVES 4.

½ pound cooked lobster meat	1 teaspoon fresh lemon juice
2 level teaspoons butter	Pinch of nutmeg
2 level teaspoons flour	1 egg, beaten
½ cup warm milk	½ cup bread crumbs
Salt and pepper, to taste	Vegetable oil, for frying

1. Finely chop the lobster meat, adding the "coral" or red roe if there is any.

2. Melt the butter and stir in the flour until well blended. Add the warm milk and whisk to a thick white sauce. Add the salt, pepper, lemon juice, and nutmeg, and mix well.

3. While the mixture is still hot, add the lobster and let it cool. When it's cool, shape into patties or small rolls.

4. Dip each croquette into the beaten egg, then into the bread crumbs, and fry in ¼ inch of oil until golden brown. Serve with cocktail or tartar sauce.

Lobster Soop

This recipe for "soop" (*sic*) appeared in the *Compleat American Housewife, Being a Collection of the Most Approved Recipes of the American Colonies*, first published in 1787.

> *Boil the knuckle of veal to a jelly strain it off—and season it as you please, put to it the body and tails of 3 lobsters a pint of white wine—make balls of the claws finely beaten and the yolks of 2 eggs, nutmeg, pepper and salt—boil them—and then fry them in butter and put them in ye soop.*

Grilled Lobster Tails with Avocado-Lime Mayonnaise

Many lobster purists resist the idea of grilling lobster, convinced that it is best boiled or steamed, period. While I am a devoted consumer of simple boiled lobster, this is a fun summer dish for a cookout.

SERVES 6.

2 ripe avocados, peeled and diced

¾ cup mayonnaise

Juice of 1 lime, or more to taste

Dash of hot sauce

Pinch of salt

3 lobsters, 1½–2 pounds each

Olive oil

Sea salt and white pepper, to taste

Lime wedges, for serving

1. Make the mayonnaise: Blend the first five ingredients until smooth. Adjust seasonings to taste and refrigerate until ready to serve.

2. Preheat a gas or charcoal grill to medium.

3. Prepare the lobsters: Parboil the lobsters for 5 to 6 minutes, and let them cool just enough that you can handle them.

4. Split the lobsters lengthwise starting between the eyes and cutting through the tail. Remove the intestines in the tail and rinse off any other debris. (A professional chef might well insist on splitting a lobster in half lengthwise while it is still alive, but for the more fainthearted among us, I suggest parboiling.)

5. Brush the lobsters with olive oil and season lightly with sea salt and white pepper.

6. Place the lobster halves shell-side down and cook for 8 to 10 minutes over medium heat, brushing with more oil several times. Turn the lobsters over for 5 minutes or so, enough to sear the meat.

7. Serve with Avocado-Lime Mayonnaise and garnish with lime wedges.

Note: This recipe is best with hard-shell lobsters. Soft-shell lobsters have too much liquid; the result is more of a poached effect.

Lobster and Asparagus Risotto with Truffle Oil

This is a luxurious combination that makes an excellent first course or lunch dish. The truffle oil adds the final sumptuous touch.

SERVES 4-6.

4 lobsters, 1–1¼ pounds each, or 1 pound lobster meat

1½ pounds asparagus

2 cups vegetable stock or lobster stock

1 cup white wine

2 cups water

1 tablespoon butter

2 tablespoons oil

2 shallots, minced

2 cups Arborio rice

Truffle oil, to taste

1. Boil the lobsters for 10 minutes or until cooked. Remove the meat, and slice the tail and knuckle meat into ½-inch pieces. Try to keep the claws whole. You can also buy ready-cooked lobster meat by the pound.

2. Break off the tough ends of the asparagus and steam for 3 to 5 minutes, depending on the size of the stalks. They should be just cooked through and still a bit crunchy. Cut into 1-inch pieces, reserving the tips.

3. Bring the stock, wine, and water just to a simmer. Keep this on the stove where you will be cooking the risotto.

4. Heat the butter and oil in a wide, heavy pot. Sauté the shallots until soft and translucent.

5. Add the Arborio rice and stir for 1 to 2 minutes, until well coated.

6. Begin adding the simmering stock ½ cup at a time. Stir the risotto each time after adding the broth until the liquid is absorbed. Cook the rice until tender but still firm, approximately 20 minutes.

7. A minute or two before the risotto is finished cooking, stir in the lobster tail and knuckle meat and pieces of asparagus stalks. Toss lightly.

8. Top each portion with a claw or piece of claw and asparagus tips. Drizzle each portion lightly with truffle oil and serve.

Lobster Mac 'n' Cheese

The usual lobster mac 'n' cheese is ubiquitous on New England menus. Some are good, some not so much. This creation is one of the best and comes from Rockland, Maine–based chef Kerry Altiero, owner of Café Miranda, its organic Headacre Farm, and author of *Adventures in Comfort Food: Incredible Delicious and New Recipes from a Unique, Small Town Restaurant.* I usually distrust the word *unique* because it is often used when "unusual" is meant, but Café Miranda is a genuine one-off.

SERVES 1-2.

4½ ounces pasta, cooked slightly past al dente

3 ounces mozzarella, shredded

1 ounce Romano or Parmesan cheese, shredded or grated

¼ cup diced fresh tomato

½ cup heavy cream

Salt and coarsely ground pepper

Dash of Marsala, port, or sherry

1 basil leaf, rolled up and thinly sliced

1½ cups loosely packed greens, such as spinach or kale
    torn into bite-size pieces, and tossed in olive oil

3 ounces cooked lobster meat

1. Preheat your oven to 350°F.

2. In a 9-inch oven-safe casserole dish, mix everything but the greens and lobster together. Bake until the sauce has become thick, 8 minutes, then sprinkle the greens over the top. Continue to bake until golden brown, another 8 minutes. By the time it is browned well, the cheese and cream will have interacted with the starch in the pasta and made a sauce that will coat a spoon.

3. When the dish is turning brown, poke the lobster pieces into the top. Just cook it for a couple of minutes after this—you don't want the lobster to turn into little erasers.

4. Want to go even further over the top? Add some raw bacon to the top of the casserole before it goes into the oven, and cook it all together.

Shrimp

"Shrimp is the fruit of the sea. You can barbeque it, boil it, broil it, bake it, sauté it. There's, um, shrimp kebabs, shrimp Creole, shrimp gumbo, pan fried, deep fried, stir fried. There's pineapple shrimp and lemon shrimp, coconut shrimp, pepper shrimp, shrimp soup, shrimp stew, shrimp salad, shrimp and potatoes, shrimp burger, shrimp sandwich. . . ."

—Bubba in *Forrest Gump*

Shrimp are one of the most globally appreciated seafoods, with major fisheries in the United States, Southeast Asia, and South America. They are an important part of many cuisines, from Japanese to Creole. There are numerous species with a variety of names, but the vast majority of what we consume are either Pacific white shrimp or giant tiger prawns. In general, the words *shrimp* and *prawn* are used interchangeably, although some people refer to larger shrimp as prawns. While the aquaculture that produces so much of the shrimp we consume is generally reliable, many of the farmed shrimp that come from places other than the U.S. (such as Southeast Asia) are not as closely monitored for health concerns and farming best practices. The Monterey Bay Aquarium Seafood Watch Guidelines suggest that best choices are U.S./Alaskan farmed shrimp. If those are unavailable, look for Canadian and U.S. wild, as well as Ecuador and Honduras farmed shrimp. Try to read the fine print on the frozen fish at the supermarket. A reputable fishmonger will generally have wholesome and sustainable varieties.

How to Peel and Devein Shrimp

To shell a shrimp, hold the tail in one hand while gently removing the shell around the body with the other. You can get rid of the tail shell altogether or leave it on for appearance and as a handy handle for dipping into cocktail sauce. To remove the vein (as in "devein the shrimp," although it is actually an intestine), make a shallow cut lengthwise down the outer curve of the shrimp's tail. Pick out the dark vein that runs lengthwise down the shrimp's back by using a pointy utensil or scraping it off with your fingertip while rinsing under running water.

The tiny Northern shrimp that were so readily available when this book was first published are now available only sporadically, due to worries about overfishing and rising water temperatures. When the fishery is open, the catch is available only for a few months in winter. The demand for these shrimp hasn't fully recovered as people became used to their absence.

Colossal shrimp (which seems like an oxymoron) is just a classification of sizes you'll find in the market. Although some providers have categories and gradients, here's the basic breakdown:

Colossal: 10 or fewer per pound
Jumbo: 11-15 per pound
Extra Large: 16-20 per pound
Large: 21-30 per pound
Medium: 31-35 per pound
Small: 36-45 per pound
Miniature: 100 per pound

For any of the recipes here, medium to small shrimp can be substituted for Northern shrimp.

Although people have been catching northern shrimp since the 1600s, there was no commercial fishery until sometime in the twentieth century. These small specimens were used primarily for bait. It wasn't until canned shrimp from the South became available that shrimp began to be a popular ingredient. Cookbooks from the early 1900s reveal little interest in shrimp. Amazing, considering the amount we now consume. And why not? Shrimp are low-cal, low fat, fast and easy to prepare, not to mention delicious.

Chilled Northern Shrimp Salad in Avocado

SERVES 6 AS AN APPETIZER.

3 ripe avocados

2 teaspoons fresh lemon juice

1 cup small cooked shrimp (or substitute crab or lobster)

⅓ cup mayonnaise

½ teaspoon grated lemon rind

½ teaspoon paprika

Salt and pepper, to taste

1. Split the avocados lengthwise and remove their pits. Brush with lemon juice to prevent them from browning.

2. In a small bowl, combine the remaining ingredients. Fill each avocado half with the shrimp mixture. Cover and chill until ready to serve.

Potted Shrimp

This is an updated New England adaptation of a popular British dish of the 1800s that was served as either an appetizer or a "savoury," which came after the main dish. Northern shrimp lend themselves well to this because they are so tender.

SERVES 4-6 AS AN HORS D'OEUVRE.

4 tablespoons softened butter, divided

3 shallots, finely chopped

½ pound northern shrimp, peeled

Salt and pepper, to taste

2 tablespoons white vermouth

½ cup cream cheese, softened

1 tablespoon fresh lemon juice

1 tablespoon chopped fresh dill

1 teaspoon Worcestershire sauce

Pinch of mace

Hot sauce, to taste

1. In a medium skillet, melt 1 tablespoon of the butter over moderate heat. Sauté the shallots until soft. Add the shrimp, along with salt and pepper to taste, and cook, stirring occasionally, until the shrimp are pink and just cooked through, about 1 to 2 minutes.

2. Add the vermouth and bring to a boil. Remove the mixture from the heat and transfer the shrimp to a cutting board. When they're cool, chop the shrimp coarsely.

3. In a bowl, blend the remaining butter and cream cheese. Stir in the shrimp, shallots, lemon juice, dill, Worcestershire sauce, and mace. Season to taste with more salt and pepper and with hot sauce. Chill for at least 4 hours. Serve with crackers.

Shrimp and Clams Cataplana

This dish is inspired by the wonderful *cataplana* dishes found in the coastal regions of Portugal, which use a copper cookpot with a hinged lid to cook shellfish with pork or sausage. By the late 1800s, there was a large Portuguese population in New England, many of whom had come to work in the thriving fisheries out of Gloucester, Fall River, and New Bedford. There are still thriving Portuguese communities in these towns. This dish is a tribute to their culinary traditions.

SERVES 4.

> 4 tablespoons olive oil, divided
>
> 1½ cups chorizo, cut in half lengthwise and then sliced
>
> 2 tablespoons chopped garlic
>
> 3 shallots, thinly sliced
>
> 1 cup sliced leeks
>
> ½ cup white wine
>
> ½ cup clam juice or fish stock
>
> 1 pound shrimp, preferably U.S. wild-caught
>
> 3 dozen littleneck clams

1. In a large pot with a tight-fitting lid or a *cataplana*, heat 2 tablespoons of the olive oil. Add the chorizo and lightly brown for about 5 minutes. Remove the chorizo and reserve.

2. Add the garlic, shallots, and leeks, and sauté until soft and golden. Add the wine and clam juice, and bring to a simmer. Add the clams, cover, and cook for 3 minutes. Add the shrimp, cover, and cook for another 2 minutes, or until the shrimp are pink and cooked through.

3. Spoon portions of clams, shrimp, and chorizo into bowls. Drizzle the remaining olive oil atop, and serve with plenty of crusty bread.

Cajun Shrimp Sauté

For this particular recipe, I prefer larger Gulf shrimp, as they are better suited to stronger, spicier flavors. This makes a great appetizer or entree served over rice. Don't be daunted by the long list of ingredients—the dish is actually quite simple. And, you can double or triple the recipe for the dry ingredients and save in an airtight jar.

SERVES 2–4.

Dry Spice

1 tablespoon chili powder

1 tablespoon dark brown sugar, firmly packed

1 teaspoon celery salt

1 teaspoon cumin

½ teaspoon white pepper

½ teaspoon dried thyme

1 teaspoon garlic powder

Shrimp

1 pound medium to large shrimp, peeled

2 tablespoons olive oil

¼ cup chopped cubanelle or poblano peppers (or substitute jalapeños or Anaheims for more heat)

⅓ cup chopped yellow onion

⅓ cup chopped scallions

¼ cup white wine

Lemon wedges, for serving

1. In a small bowl, mix together the dry ingredients. Toss the shrimp in this mixture to coat.

2. In a large skillet, heat the olive oil. Add the peppers, onion, and scallions, and sauté until soft. Add the shrimp and wine, and cook over medium heat until the shrimp are pink and firm, about 3 to 4 minutes. Serve hot with lemon wedges.

Shrimp Bisque

You can use just about any smaller shrimp, but if you can find whole, head-on northern shrimp, especially if they are fresh and not frozen, grab them! This isn't essential, but the heads add extra flavor to the stock.

Although this dish is somewhat labor intensive, the final product is a delicate bisque that will reward your efforts. It makes a lovely cold-weather lunch or supper with a green salad and crusty bread.

SERVES 6-8.

2 pounds small shrimp, heads and shells on

1 cup white wine or dry vermouth

2 cups water, divided

1 bay leaf

3 tablespoons butter, divided

1 tablespoon olive oil

⅓ cup chopped celery

⅓ cup chopped shallots

⅓ cup chopped carrots

2 tablespoons flour

2 tablespoons tomato paste

1 teaspoon sea salt

½ teaspoon white pepper

½ teaspoon Old Bay Seasoning

¼ teaspoon dry mustard

1 pint (2 cups) light cream

2 tablespoons sherry

1. Remove the heads from the shrimp and reserve.

2. Heat the wine, bayleaf, and 1 cup of the water in a large pot. Bring to a boil. Add the shrimp tails. Reduce the heat and simmer for 2 minutes. Remove the shrimp from the liquid and plunge into cold water to cool. When they're cool, remove the shells.

3. In the same pot, melt 1 tablespoon of the butter. Add the olive oil, heat through, then add the celery, shallots, and carrots. Sauté until soft, about 7 minutes,

4. Return the shells, the reserved shrimp heads, and the liquid to the pot and simmer over low heat for 20 minutes.

5. Strain the liquid though a colander, pressing on the solids.

6. In a saucepan, melt remaining 2 tablespoons of butter. Whisk in the flour to make a roux. Cook over very low heat for 4 to 5 minutes, being careful not to burn.

7. Whisk in the shrimp stock and simmer over low heat for about 5 minutes, until thick and smooth. Add the tomato paste, salt, pepper, Old Bay Seasoning, and dry mustard. Whisk in the cream and sherry and heat through, about a minute. Do not let the soup boil. Serve immediately.

Wild Mushroom and Shrimp Linguine

This is a very quick dish that can be made with any small shrimp. Adjust the garlic up or down to your taste. Serve with crusty bread and a salad for a quick and healthy dinner.

SERVES 4–6.

> 1 pound linguine
>
> ¼ cup olive oil
>
> 4 cloves garlic, minced
>
> 2 leeks, halved, rinsed, and thinly sliced
>
> ½ pound mixed "wild" mushrooms, such as oyster, cremini, or shiitake, cleaned and sliced
>
> 1 pound small shrimp, shelled
>
> 1 tablespoon thinly sliced basil

1. Cook pasta according to the package directions.

2. While the linguine is cooking, heat the olive oil in a large pot or deep skillet. Add the garlic and leeks and sauté over low heat until soft and golden. Add the mushrooms and sauté until soft and shiny.

3. Add the shrimp and cook until just cooked through, about 2 minutes.

4. Drain the pasta, reserving ½ cup of the pasta water. Add the linguine to the shrimp-mushroom mixture. Stir well, adding enough of the pasta water to create a thin sauce. Top with basil and serve immediately.

Barbecued Shrimp Skewers

This recipe is best done with larger shrimp. They hold up to grilling or broiling better, and their slightly stronger flavor pairs well with flavorful marinades like this one.

SERVES 4–6 AS AN HORS D'OEUVRE.

½ cup olive oil

⅓ cup soy sauce

2 tablespoons rice wine vinegar

1 tablespoon brown sugar

1 tablespoon minced garlic

1 teaspoon sesame oil

1 teaspoon grated orange rind

1 pound large shrimp, shells split lengthwise but left on

Lemon wedges, for serving

1. Combine all the ingredients except the shrimp and lemon wedges in a small bowl. Whisk until well combined.

2. In a glass dish or resealable plastic bag, marinate the shrimp in this mixture for at least 30 minutes and up to 2 hours.

3. Thread the shrimp onto metal or bamboo skewers that have been soaked in water to prevent scorching.

4. Grill over medium heat for about 2 minutes per side, or until the shrimp are firm and pink. Serve warm or at room temperature with lemon wedges.

Fin Fish

"It's no fish ye're buying, it's men's lives."

—Sir Walter Scott

This section is devoted to "swimming" fish, or more accurately fin fish (since some shell-fish can swim). I've focused primarily on fish that are relatively common in the Northeast. In many ways the history of the New England fisheries is the history of New England. The first settlers may have come to escape religious oppression, but the subsequent story of survival—and success—is one very big fish story.

When the first settlers arrived, they found a native population that embraced fish and shellfish as a wonderful and plentiful source of food. The bounty of the sea was fresh, nutritious, and relatively easy to harvest. Fish and shellfish were often the centerpiece of

New England tribal gatherings and celebrations. But for the Europeans, fish came with the historical baggage of being associated with fast days, Lenten deprivation, and a rather meager substitute for "real" food like beef and pork. (We now know that not only is fish one of the best sources of protein available to us, but it's also low in calories, low in fat, and offers other health benefits.) The fact that seafood was enjoyed so richly by the Native American tribes only strengthened the settlers' prejudices, because it became known as Indian food. It was not until the 1800s that the non-Native population would begin to view seafood as the incredible gift it is.

When Captain John Smith and others first explored New England waters, they didn't find gold or spices, but they did find an abundance of fish, particularly codfish that had been caught, salted and dried by earlier Europeans who then returned home with their long-lasting staple. These fishing boats predate permanent settlements on the mainland, and there is evidence of their seasonal presence off the coast of Maine and New Hampshire. Reporting back to England, these intrepid seafarers described the teeming waters they sailed, and the possibilities were not lost on English investors. Soon transatlantic fishing trips were a common occurrence, and in time New England replaced Newfoundland as the preferred fishing ground.

Since cod could be salted and dried, it became a long-lived staple, and much of the British catch was sold to Portugal and Spain, where the demand for *bacalao* was perpetual. In the 1700s, the sugarcane industry was built on the backs of slaves fed on salt cod. Dried fish of inferior quality was sold to sugarcane plantations in the Caribbean and fed to slaves.

Today our fishing boats are working harder and harder, and we are eating more fish than ever: 16.6 pounds per capita in 2004, up from 11.5 pounds in 1910. The U.S. fishery brings in some 9.6 billion pounds a year. Sound like a lot? Actually, the United States ranks fifth in total annual catch, behind China, Peru, India, and Indonesia. Sadly, our supplies are diminishing and our exports increasing. We can only hope that, with luck and proper management, our fisheries will not go the way of some of the Scandinavian countries, where abundant catches are only a memory and once prosperous fishing villages are nearly abandoned.

Future abundance may well depend on our ability to perfect aquaculture and to broaden our tastes so that underused species can add diversity to our diets. Fish that have been used widely in Europe are now gaining popularity thanks to a generation of inventive new chefs, many of whom are in the Northeast.

How to Choose Good Fish

When it comes to seafood, the nose always knows. Any fish that smells "fishy" is not something you want to take home. Good fresh fish has very little smell except for a briny, oceany scent. Any hint of ammonia or off-smell means the fish is past its sell-by date. Most fish are more readily available in steaks or fillets than whole. When choosing these, look for firm, moist pieces. A dry appearance or dull color usually means a second-rate product.

If you have the opportunity to choose a whole fish, look for bright clear eyes and red gills, as opposed to gray or brown, another indicator of age. Most New England fish markets that have been around for any length of time will stock only quality seafoods, but it's always okay to ask what's best on that day or what has come in most recently. It sounds weird, but don't be afraid to ask to smell the fish, too. I have a few local sources that I use, and developing a relationship with your fishmonger is a surefire way to get the freshest and the best.

The dangers of eating certain kinds of fish have been flashed about a lot lately, but it would be a shame to avoid fish and all its health benefits because of worries about mercury. The fact is that the primary concerns are for pregnant women, babies, and young children. According to the Environmental Protection Agency, "Research shows that most people's fish consumption does not cause a health concern. However, high levels of mercury in the bloodstream of unborn babies and young children may harm the developing nervous system. With this in mind, FDA and EPA designed an advisory that if followed should keep an individual's mercury consumption below levels that have been shown to cause harm. By following the advisory, parents can be confident of reducing their unborn or young child's exposure to the harmful effects of mercury, while at the same time maintaining a healthy diet that includes the nutritional benefits of fish and shellfish." If you are concerned, please visit www.epa.gov, and look under "Fish Consumption Advisories" in the "Mercury" section.

"It would be better for the health of those who do not labor, if they would use more fish and less flesh for food. But then fish cannot be rendered so palatable, because it does not admit the variety of cooking and flavors that other animal food does."

—*Early American Cookery: The Good Housekeeper*
by Sarah Josepha Hale (1841)

A Note on Sustainability

In the interest of broadening seafood horizons, some recipes here call for fish that are native to the North Atlantic, but are less common commercially than the usual cod–haddock–swordfish lineup. Since I first wrote this book 12 years ago, we've watched so many of our fisheries dwindle away. Fortunately, with proper management, some have been revived. In general, smaller fish, those further down the marine food chain, tend to be higher in omega-3 oils and are less likely to have significant levels of mercury or other toxins. One of the main health benefits of the Mediterranean diet is eating a wide variety of seafood. In markets in other parts of the world, you'll find an array of seafood that we might well not recognize: scabbard fish, mullet, anglerfish, herring, eels, and more.

To help us choose the best seafood, the Monterey Bay Aquarium in Monterey, California, publishes the *SeafoodWatch Guide,* updated every six months. There is a very handy, printable, wallet-sized guide on their website.

The North Atlantic Marine Alliance, an organization devoted to both sustainable seafood and preserving small fisheries, provides these seven guidelines for choosing fish.

1. Buy from local fishermen whenever possible.

2. Choose seafood that has traveled the least distance.

3. Choose wild seafood whenever possible.

4. Avoid farmed finfish and shrimp.

5. Avoid fake or imitation seafood products.

6. Get involved in a Community Supported Fishery (CSF).

7. Ask how, where, and when your seafood was caught.

Even with guidelines like these, what types of seafood to eat or not to eat is a complicated matter, and there are varying opinions on what is sustainable and what is not. The variables include how fish are caught, where they are caught, whether they are farmed or not. If certain varieties are farmed, it can make a difference how and where the farming is done. I have not listed specific types of fish as sustainable because the lists change faster than a book can. But fundamentally, the more we come to accept and enjoy different types of fish, the more likely we are to have strong, sustainable fisheries.

A Note on the Recipes

I've tried to provide a range of recipes, from historic to cutting edge. In my own recipes, my goal has been to keep things simple to let the flavors of the fish shine through. In my conversations with chefs, this is something that kept coming up, though some of their preparations are more complex than anything I could have dreamed up on my own.

One of the biggest challenges in writing this book was creating recipes. Since I generally don't cook using recipes, it was difficult to remember to measure and time things. I hope most of them are clear, but I urge you to experiment according to your own tastes. And by all means, substitute clams for mussels, cod for haddock, swordfish for halibut. Generally, you can substitute any firm fish steak for any other, and any mild white fillets for any other. Get creative!

You'll notice, too, a broad range of ethnic influences which should come as no surprise. The New England fisheries have attracted people from countries like Spain, Portugal, the Azores, Italy, Scandinavia, and Cape Verde (to name a few) since this country was founded. It's natural—and wonderful—that there are so many cultural influences to keep things interesting.

Bass

No angling can surpass
The taking of the Basse

—Anonymous

In mid-nineteenth century southern New England, fishing for bass was a favorite summer pastime. Excursion boats took residents of the sweltering cities out for a day of fishing on Long Island Sound or the Atlantic. In New York City, these boats came complete with a live band and cotillion parties on the upper deck. Along with fishing for bass (and other fish), the entertainment included a stop at Coney Island for a swim and a clambake.

Today bass fishing is, if anything, even more popular here, not least because the fish are both fine sport and delicious eating. Two particular species of bass are most commonly targeted: the striped bass and the black sea bass.

Striped Bass

Sitting at my desk on a July morning, I can see the striped bass fishermen in the cove. There is a boat with a few guys in it fishing on light tackle or fly rods. They nudge the boat as close to the rocks as they dare and cast their lines in long, graceful arcs. Anglers on the rocks or beach are casting with heavier gear. On the nearby bridges over the Portsmouth Harbor estuaries, there are fishermen oblivious to the passing cars, focused only on hooking a fierce-fighting striper big enough to keep.

In most places July Fourth is celebrated by cookouts and fireworks. Around here it's also fishing for stripers.

The American Angler's Guide of 1849 is unequivocal in its appreciation of the striped bass: "This noble and highly prized fish is peculiar to our own country, and to particular parts of it. As an object of sport, for perfect symmetry and beauty of appearance, and as a dish for the table, it is considered second only to the salmon."

Striped bass are not related to another Atlantic bass—the black sea bass—but are of the same family as mackerel and bluefish. As with these cousins, stripers' flesh is somewhat oily, so they should be put on ice as soon as they're caught; they're best eaten within twenty-four hours. Although anglers love to hook really big fish, the best ones for the table are less than 10 pounds.

Striped bass used to be more than plentiful, as the Pilgrims aboard the *Mayflower* enthusiastically attested. Overfishing and pollution put the species at risk, and while there is still a commercial fishery, the catch has been much reduced in recent decades. Aquaculturists, however, have crossed the striped bass and the white bass and are now raising considerable numbers of farmed "striped bass."

Black Sea Bass

The black sea bass is a wonderful fish for the table, with mild white flesh. Most of the fish are around a pound and a half—a good size for cooking whole.

Color is not the only unusual thing about black sea bass. They are protogynous hermaphrodites, which means that initially they are females, but some larger fish (between 9 and 13 inches) reverse sex to become males, the reversal usually taking place after spawning. Stripers are also protogynous hermaphrodites, but their sexual reversal is the opposite of black bass: male to female.

The black sea bass population is considered to be in pretty good shape in New England and the Mid-Atlantic states. South of that, the species is regarded as overfished.

Sea bass (sometimes the *black* is omitted in their name) may not be as fierce as stripers or bluefish, but pound for pound they make fine sport on light tackle.

Salt-Crusted Black Sea Bass

This recipe is a personal favorite of Joachim Sandbichler, a veteran restaurateur, who currently owns and manages Patio in Provincetown, Massachusetts. Austrian-born Sandbichler used to spend his summers on the Italian coast, where *branzino*, or Mediterranean sea bass, was often served this way. Black sea bass makes a great North Atlantic substitute. Joachim serves this with a simple arugula or tomato salad.

SERVES 2.

> 1 (2-pound) black sea bass, gutted and cleaned, leaving head and tail intact
> 1 lemon, sliced into rounds
> 4 sprigs tarragon or other fresh herbs
> Salt and pepper, to taste
> 2 cups kosher or coarse sea salt
> 2 cups flour
> 1 cup warm water
> 2 tablespoons extra-virgin olive oil

1. Preheat the oven to 400°F.

2. Clean the fish and pat it dry. Place the lemon slices and herbs in the cavity of the cleaned fish; salt and pepper to taste.

3. In a bowl, combine the salt, flour, and water. You should be able to form balls that stay together briefly before falling apart.

4. Place a 1-inch-thick layer of the salt paste on the bottom of a baking dish slightly larger than the fish.

5. Rub the bass on all sides with the olive oil. Place the fish on top of the salt layer, and put the rest of the salt and flour mixture on top. Firmly pack it around the fish.

6. Place the fish in the oven and roast for about 30 minutes. Remove the fish and allow it to cool slightly. Remove the salt crust and serve hot.

Striped Bass with Julienned Vegetables and Red Pepper Coulis

This great recipe comes from award-winning chef Leo Bushey, a Connecticut native son.

SERVES 4.

Coulis

1 (8-ounce) jar roasted red peppers

1 medium potato, peeled and cut into ½-inch dice

1 carrot, peeled and chopped

2 cloves garlic, peeled

1 medium yellow onion, chopped

3–4 (8-ounce) bottles clam juice

Fish and Vegetables

1 carrot, peeled

1 medium summer squash, halved lengthwise and seeded

1 medium zucchini, halved lengthwise and seeded

1 tablespoon canola oil

1½ pounds skin-on striped bass fillets, cut into 4 equal pieces

Salt and pepper, to taste

1 tablespoon butter

1 shallot, finely chopped

1. Put all of the coulis ingredients into a stockpot and simmer for about an hour. Remove from the heat and allow to cool slightly.

2. In a blender or food processor, blend the mixture until smooth. Pour the coulis into a smaller saucepan, and keep warm.

3. Next, cut the carrot, summer squash, and zucchini into 2-inch lengths and then julienne into thin lengthwise strips.

4. In a skillet, heat the canola oil over medium-high heat until it's hot but not smoking. Season the fillets with salt and pepper and add to the pan.

5. Cook for 2 to 3 minutes on each side, until the skin is crisp and the fish just cooked through.

6. Remove the fillets to a platter and keep them warm. Wipe out the skillet with a paper towel.

7. Add the butter to the pan and melt over medium-high heat. Add the julienned vegetables and shallot. Stir-fry for 1 to 2 minutes or until just crisp-tender.

8. To serve, spread equal portions of the warm coulis on each plate, top with fish, and then top with the vegetables.

Baked Striped Bass with Bacon

This recipe is adapted from one that appears on the website for Reelin Sportfishing Charters, which operates out of New London, Connecticut. Their site has an archive of recipes for various kinds of sportfish. I thought this was a particularly interesting way to prepare striped bass.

SERVES 4.

> 4 (6- to 8-ounce) striped bass fillets
>
> 1 quart golden ginger ale (or substitute 1 pint white wine and 1 pint water with a tablespoon of grated fresh ginger)
>
> 4 pieces thick-sliced bacon
>
> 1 cup sliced baby portobello or cremini mushrooms
>
> 1 cup red onion, sliced
>
> 4 tablespoons butter
>
> ¼ teaspoon dried tarragon
>
> Dash of paprika

1. Soak the bass overnight in the ginger ale in the refrigerator. Rinse when you're ready to cook. Preheat the oven to 350°F.

2. In a pan, cook the bacon until crisp. Remove the bacon from the pan and drain on paper towels. Crumble the bacon and set aside. Cook the mushrooms and onion in the bacon fat until tender.

3. Place the fish in a baking dish. Combine the mushrooms, onion, butter, and tarragon. Spread on top of the fish; sprinkle with paprika. Bake for approximately 20 minutes, until the fish flakes easily. Garnish with the crumbled bacon.

Cod

A reunion of the cod family would be quite a gathering. It would include haddock, hake, pollock, cusk, scrod, and tomcod, along with such preparations as salt cod, kedgeree, and finnan haddie.

The Atlantic cod is, of course, the pater familias, and some of the rest of the family suffer by comparison.

Haddock is the second most popular of the cod family. It closely resembles the cod, although it is usually gray with a black patch on its side; the cod has a brownish cast. From a culinary point of view, haddock is almost interchangeable with cod, although it's thought to be less appropriate for salting. Haddock is, however, the preferred fish for finnan haddie, which is split, smoked haddock; *haddie* is Scottish slang for "haddock." But the problem with both of these species is that, due to our rather narrow tastes in fish, ground fish stocks have been seriously depleted. I urge you to try some of the codfish cousins whenever possible. I'm betting that if I invited you for dinner and served you cusk instead of cod, you wouldn't notice, unless your palate is more evolved than mine.

Hake's problem, at least in the United States, is that it needs better publicity. Oddly enough, this has been tried by renaming the hake to something that might sound more appealing, including whiting, whitefish, Pacific whiting, and ling. Nothing has really worked, and typically the price of hake is about half that of cod. The meat is much like cod, though a little firmer textured.

In Europe, hake is more highly regarded and appears under its own name on menus at expensive restaurants. At the same time, Gorton's excellent *Fish Glossary* says that hake "provides many countries with a good inexpensive source of protein." A noble calling to be sure but not haute cuisine.

Pollock and now dogfish (not part of the family) are the species of choice for frozen fish, fish sticks, and fish-and-chips—but that doesn't mean that it isn't a good substitute for cod. Indeed, this common usage may be only a reflection of tradition and the fact that pollock is still abundant and easier to catch than cod. Pollock flesh is firm and may be grayer than cod. Its high fat content lends a slightly stronger taste than cod. Pollock are popular with recreational fishermen, as they are caught in shallower waters than cod and are stronger fighters. Cod, on the other hand, seem to take a more fatalistic view of being caught by rod and reel.

Cusk is the odd-looking member of the family, with its full-length dorsal fin and small eyes. It's becoming more popular as a culinary substitute for the more expensive cod, but much of the catch is still salted or goes into frozen food as "white fish."

The tomcod looks like an immature cod but is actually a smaller variety—most are less than 12 inches long. Tomcod are voracious eaters and provide good sport for inshore anglers. They're highly prized for their delicate flavor.

Although a popular New England menu item, *scrod* is really only a culinary term for a young member of the cod family. It could be any one of the above species.

Fish Chowder

I include this chowder recipe here because cod—given its historic abundance—has long been a popular chowder fish. You could, however, use any firm white-fleshed fish, including hake or cusk. I tend to prefer these to halibut (too expensive for chowder, in my view), and to flounder and sole, which are a bit too delicate for the soup pot. At any rate, fish chowder recipes seem to have changed very little over the years.

SERVES 6–8.

    2 slices thick-cut bacon, or 2 tablespoons diced salt pork

    5 medium potatoes cut into ½-inch chunks

    1 large onion, chopped

    2 cups fish stock or water

    1½ pounds cod, cut into 1-inch pieces

    1 pint light cream

    1 (12-ounce) can evaporated skim milk

    Salt and pepper, to taste

1. In a frying pan, cook the bacon or salt pork until it's browned and its fat is rendered. Pour off all but 2 tablespoons of fat.

2. Add the potatoes and onion to the pan, and cook in the fat until the onion is translucent. Add fish stock or water to cover and simmer for 10 minutes.

3. Add the cod and simmer for another 5 to 10 minutes, or until the fish is cooked through.

4. Add the cream and evaporated milk and heat through. Season to taste. Serve very hot with a dab of butter added to each bowl, if desired.

Kedgeree

This is an old-time recipe for cod that probably originated with English settlers and fishermen. It is adapted for today's cooks in *A Taste of History: 19th Century Food of Mystic Seaport.*

SERVES 6–8.

  2 tablespoons butter

  2 tablespoons flour

  2 cups milk

  4 finely chopped hard-boiled egg yolks (whites, optional)

  Salt and pepper, to taste

  2 cups cooked white rice

  1 cup cooked, flaked codfish

1. Preheat the oven to 350°F.

2. Make a white sauce: Melt the butter in a saucepan over medium heat. Whisk in the flour and cook until a smooth paste forms. Whisk in the milk and stir until thickened. Add the yolks, salt, and pepper.

3. Add the cooked rice and fish, and toss until well blended, adding more sauce if needed. Put into a greased casserole dish or baking pan. (Options: Season with nutmeg or mace; top with buttered cracker crumbs.)

4. Bake until hot and bubbling, about 8-10 minutes.

Roast Cod with Potato-Horseradish Crust

SERVES 4.

- 2 medium baking potatoes, grated
- 1 shallot, finely minced
- 1 egg white, beaten
- 2 tablespoons horseradish
- Salt and pepper, to taste
- 1½ pounds cod fillets, divided into 4 portions
- 2 tablespoons mayonnaise
- 1 tablespoon vegetable oil

1. Preheat the oven to 425°F.

2. In a clean dishtowel, squeeze any excess liquid from the grated potatoes. In a small bowl, combine the potatoes, shallot, egg white, and horseradish. Mix well.

3. Salt and pepper the cod to taste. Spread the mayonnaise on the cod fillets and top with the potato mixture.

4. Heat the oil in a frying pan, and carefully place the cod fillets, potato-side down, into the pan. Fry until the potatoes are golden.

5. Place the fish potato-side up in a baking dish, and bake for 10 to 12 minutes or until the fish is opaque and flaky.

Oven-Roasted Cod with Lobster, Corn, Potato, and Cream

This wonderful entree from chef Valerie Lareau, who, years ago, was the chef at Robert's Maine Grill in Kittery, Maine, takes classic New England ingredients and gives them a simple but elegant spin.

SERVES 2.

> 1 russet potato
>
> ½ cup rendered duck fat or bacon fat
>
> Pinch of sea salt
>
> Pinch of black pepper
>
> 1 (1½-pound) lobster, cooked
>
> 1 ear corn
>
> 12 ounces fresh cod fillets, cut into 2 portions
>
> ½ cup heavy cream

1. Preheat the oven to 400°F. Shred the potato and hold in a bowl of cold water.

2. Melt the duck fat or bacon fat in a heavy skillet.

3. Drain the potato and squeeze out any excess water. Spread evenly in the hot skillet and let brown. Salt and pepper lightly. When it's brown, drain on a paper towel.

4. Pick the meat out of the cooked lobster and slice.

5. Shuck the corn. Cut the kernels from the cob and set aside.

6. Place the cod portions in an ovenproof pan; salt and pepper to taste. Lay the potato, corn, and lobster loosely on top of the fish, then add the heavy cream to the pan. Bake for 15 minutes or until just opaque and flaky.

Baked Cod with Shallots and Lemon

This is a homey recipe that has been around for some time in various incarnations. I like it because it doesn't need a lot of exotic ingredients and is simple and quick.

SERVES 6.

1 cup mayonnaise

½ cup grated Parmesan cheese

4 tablespoons white Worcestershire sauce

3 tablespoons fresh lemon juice

Salt and pepper, to taste

2 pounds cod fillets

2 shallots, thinly sliced

1 lemon, thinly sliced

1. Preheat the oven to 400°F.

2. Mix the mayonnaise, Parmesan, Worcestershire, and lemon juice in a small bowl. Salt and pepper the fish to taste, then spread the cheese mixture atop the cod fillets.

3. Place three or four slices of shallot and of lemon on top of the mixture. Bake the cod for 20 minutes, or until it's opaque and flakes easily.

Salt Cod

Salt cod is one of the great examples of necessity being the mother of invention. The original function of salting cod—or other fish, for that matter—was to preserve it for future use. Fresh fish has a very short shelf life, and even iced fish (ice being itself a precious commodity before electricity) doesn't last very long. Salted and dried fish, however, lasted the weeks and months it took to get from the fishing grounds in the New World back to Europe on a sailing vessel and then to market.

The first Europeans who came to New England caught cod, salted it, dried it on wooden racks ("flakes"), and sailed it back to Europe. At first they came in the spring and returned with their salted cod in the fall. In the mid-1600s, fishermen began to winter over in places like the Isles of Shoals, New Hampshire. These fishermen became the first European inhabitants of New England. All for salt cod.

What is amazing about salt cod now, even in the age of refrigeration and freezing, is that it has much more than a nostalgic place in many cuisines. Its flavor and texture continue to be highly valued long after its original purpose has disappeared.

The basics of salting cod are quite simple. The cleaned fish is packed with coarse salt, layer upon layer, either in a barrel or in the open air. The weight of the many layers of salt and cod helps force out more of the moisture. After 10 days to 3 weeks, depending upon temperature and humidity, any loose salt and debris are removed, and the salted cod is set on flakes to dry. The waterfront of fishing towns used to be dominated by salt flakes. You can see a small section of flakes today at Mystic Seaport.

The air-drying fish are sometimes shaded against too much sun. In New England, however, they're more often covered by tarps against rain and fog.

The fascinating short film *A Hard Racket for Living*—made in 1948 and available for view on the Internet—shows the cod-salting process in Newfoundland and Labrador.

For connoisseurs of salt cod, a number of different cure recipes are available, ranging from a mild cure with relatively low salt content to a more intense version ("high cured") with double the amount of salt. A mild-cured fish is usually somewhat flexible and off-white in color. The rock-hard salt cod we usually see in our supermarkets is high cured.

If salt cod is not available in your area, you can approximate a mild cure by packing a cleaned cod in coarse salt (using a glass container) and leaving it in the fridge for about three days—or you can use the same technique for seven to ten days in the open air. Every few days, check to see that there are no air spaces between the salted fish.

Traditional Jamaican Salt Cod

This recipe appeared in the *Jamaica Cookery Book* in 1893 and is still considered one of the national dishes of Jamaica. It's the kind of dish that probably provided sustenance to slaves laboring in the cane fields who were fed on inferior salted cod caught in the waters off New England.

Ackee is a tropical fruit with texture resembling scrambled eggs. The flesh of the seedpods is edible when ripe (indeed, the seeds are toxic, as the cookbook writer points out) and has a mild sweetness that contrasts with the saltiness of the cod. The salt cod would have been soaked in several changes of water to make it possible to cook.

One pound of salt fish
The fruit of twelve ackee pods
Lard
Butter
Black pepper

Soak the salt fish overnight. Put it on to boil in cold water; otherwise it hardens. Throw off the first water and put it on again to boil. Carefully pick the ackees free from all red inside, which is dangerous, and boil them for about twenty minutes; add them to the salt fish which is then cut in small pieces; add some lard, butter and pepper. Some prefer the salt fish and ackees mashed together and the melted lard and butter poured over the top.

Salt Cod Cakes with Chili-Lime Mayonnaise

This is an updated twist on a very old recipe. Salt cod and potatoes could historically be kept for a long period of time, making this a popular combination. You could also make this with leftover fresh cod and leftover mashed potatoes.

MAKES 8 FISH CAKES OR 24 HORS D'OEUVRE PORTIONS.

1 pound salt cod	½ cup diced scallions
1 whole lime, sliced into wedges	Zest of 1 whole lime
2 medium potatoes	Juice of 1 lime
2 cloves garlic, sliced	1 teaspoon chili-garlic sauce
4 tablespoons olive oil	½ cup good-quality mayonnaise
⅓ cup diced bell pepper	⅓ cup plain yogurt

1. First, prepare the salt cod for cooking: Brush any extra salt off the cod fillets and rinse them well under running water. Place them in a glass dish and cover with water. Refrigerate for 24 hours, rinsing and changing the water three times during that period.

2. Rinse one last time and place in a large saucepan with a cover. Place the sliced lime wedges atop the fillets.

3. Add water to cover. Simmer, covered, for 8 to 10 minutes, or until the fish flakes easily in your hands.

4. Next, make the fish cakes: Peel and chop the potatoes. Place them in a saucepan and add the sliced garlic. Simmer for 15 minutes or until the potatoes are soft. Drain thoroughly and mash.

5. In a sauté pan, heat 1 tablespoon of the olive oil. Add the pepper and scallions and sauté until just soft.

6. In a bowl, combine the cod, mashed potatoes, and sautéed vegetables; mix well. The mixture should be sticky enough to form into cakes with your hands. Form into patties or cakes about 3 inches in diameter for an entree or 1 inch for hors d'oeuvre size.

7. Heat another tablespoon of the olive oil in a frying pan and fry the cakes until golden brown on each side, adding more oil as necessary. Drain on paper towels and keep warm.

8. Finally, make the mayonnaise: Combine the lime zest, lime juice, chili-garlic sauce, mayonnaise, and yogurt in a nonreactive bowl. Chill and serve with the cod cakes.

Flounder

Flounder are part of a large family of flatfish that are found in both the Atlantic and the Pacific. They are closely related to other flatfish, including the largest bottom dweller, halibut, and the tiny, delicate sand dabs that may weigh as little as 6 ounces. But there's a good deal of confusion when it comes to identifying flounder, as opposed to sole, dab, or plaice. Suffice it to say they are all delicious and lend themselves to a wide variety of cooking methods.

In New England, the most common species are winter flounder—which, to continue the confusion, is often marketed as lemon sole—and summer flounder, also known as fluke. Summer flounder are found in sandy harbors and bays and come in a variety of mottled browns and grays. They can camouflage themselves to some degree to blend in with their environment.

Winter flounder range from Labrador to the coasts of the Carolinas, but they're most common along the North Atlantic. According to Captain Dave, a Boston-based charter captain, angler, and saltwater fish expert, "In New England, flounder reproduce in estuaries from January to May, with peak activity in February and March when the water temperatures are the coldest of the year. Evidence suggests that individual fish

Fishing for Doormats

One of my favorite summer pastimes when I was a little girl was flounder fishing. You hear flounder referred to as doormats for their tendency to just sit on the ocean floor like, well, a doormat. It wasn't exactly sport fishing—more just a matter of pulling them off the bottom. We'd anchor the skiff 50 yards or so offshore and drop anchor. I had my own hand line with one small hook and a lead weight attached. I can still remember the smell of the tar used to coat the line so it wouldn't rot away.

If we were fishing with pieces of clams, I could bait my own hook, but when it came to sea worms, it was a job for Dad. (I bait my own hook these days, but truth be told, I'd still rather have someone else do it.) Then it was a matter of choosing which side of the boat to fish on. Most of the time we could see the bottom, and once our eyes adjusted, we'd sometimes catch the slight sandy motion of a flounder rippling across the seafloor. We plunked the bait in front of the fish until he decided it was his next meal.

Then he became *our* next meal—home to Mom, who never complained about the cleaning and gutting. She'd serve our flounder pan-fried, sometimes with homemade french fries and always with tartar sauce. On a good day, we'd bring home six or eight fish—a feast for our small family. I still think that if anyone who claims they don't like fish had it this fresh and this deliciously prepared, they'd become converts.

return for many years to the same site to spawn. . . ." And Captain Dave is no stranger to the culinary aspects of flounder. As he says, "Few fish lend themselves to more imaginative dishes as does winter flounder. Its texture and delicate flavor are well suited to sauces, spices, fruit, vegetables, and other seafood. Few things can be mixed with so many things and still stand out." In fact, *Larousse Gastronomique*, the bible of classic French cooking, lists no fewer than twenty-six different preparations for sole. I've only included a few in this chapter, but try inventing your own sauces, seasoning blends, and stuffings. It's hard to go wrong.

Jasper White's Pan-Roasted Whole Flounder or Fluke with Brown Butter, Lemon, and Capers

Chef Jasper is one of the most renowned seafood chefs in the country, and in New England he is legendary. He is the author of four cookbooks and the founder of the Summer Shack restaurants. The recipe below comes from his book *The Summer Shack Cookbook.* He tells us, "If you or a friend catch a few nice medium-sized flounder or fluke, you owe it to yourself to cook some on the bone—it is by far the best way to experience the full flavor and juiciness of the fish. This is a special dish, beautiful to behold and perfect for a quiet dinner for two."

Author's note: I'm thinking, "Date night!"

SERVES 2.

> 1 (1- to 1½-pound) whole fluke or flounder, preferably skinned by the fish market
>
> ¾ cup all-purpose flour
>
> Kosher or sea salt
>
> Freshly ground black pepper
>
> ¼ cup vegetable oil
>
> 4 tablespoons unsalted butter
>
> 1 tablespoon fresh lemon juice
>
> 1 tablespoon capers, rinsed
>
> 1 tablespoon chopped fresh Italian parsley
>
> Pinch of salt

1. If necessary, skin the fish: Start by cutting off the head. Then make a little V-cut at the tail in order to loosen the skin enough to get a firm grip on it. Peel the skin back far enough to get your thumb under the loose skin. To prevent slipping, hold a towel in your hand as you grip the skin. In one strong, swift motion, pull the skin away from the tail—it should come off in one piece. Flip the fish over and remove the skin from the other side. Then trim the small bones away from the sides of the fish, and remove the roe sac (if any) and any viscera from the cavity. If necessary, cut off the tail of the fish so that it will fit into your pan. Rinse and dry the fish. Keep refrigerated until you are ready to cook.

2. Adjust a rack to the lower third of the oven and preheat the oven to 400°F.

3. Place a 12-inch well-seasoned skillet over high heat and heat for 5 minutes. Meanwhile, spread the flour in a large shallow bowl or a baking dish. Sprinkle the fish generously with salt and pepper and dredge it in the flour, turning it well to coat; shake gently to remove the excess.

4. Add the oil to the hot skillet. Lower the fish into the skillet and reduce the heat to medium-high (at this point, you should start cooking the butter; see step 5). Brown the fish on one side without turning, about 4 minutes. Turn the fish and immediately place the skillet in the oven. Roast until the fish is pure white and firm to the touch, about 8 minutes. Transfer the fish to a platter and keep warm.

5. Meanwhile, as soon as the fish goes into the pan, place the butter in an 8-inch skillet and melt it over medium-low heat. Reduce the heat to low and cook the butter gently until it browns—keep an eye on it, but let it cook undisturbed until it is nutty brown. This will take about 8 minutes (about the same time it takes to cook the fish). When the butter is nutty brown, remove the skillet from the heat and immediately add the lemon juice, capers, parsley, and a pinch of salt. Pour the still-foaming butter into a sauceboat or serving bowl and spoon just a bit over the fish.

6. Present the fish at the table and allow a minute for your guest to admire it. To fillet the fish, hold an ordinary tablespoon upside down in the center of the fish, near the head, and loosen the top fillet, pushing out from the center of the fish. The bones on a flounder are very strong and won't pull away with the meat. You should have no problem removing the two fillets on the top side. Transfer them to a dinner plate. Flip the fish over and repeat with the two remaining fillets. Spoon the brown butter over the fish and enjoy this special treat, noticing how much more flavorful fish is when cooked on the bone.

Crab-Stuffed Flounder Roulades

This is a quick and easy preparation that is definitely good enough for a dinner party.

SERVES 2.

12 ounces fresh or frozen crabmeat

1 tablespoon mayonnaise

1 tablespoon diced shallots

1 tablespoon sliced fresh chives

4 (4- to 5-ounce) flounder fillets

2 tablespoons olive oil

Salt and pepper, to taste

1. Preheat the oven to 450°F.

2. In a bowl, combine the crabmeat, mayonnaise, shallots, and chives.

3. Cut the flounder fillets in half lengthwise on their side, cut-side down. Place a tablespoon or more of the crab mixture on each strip and roll up.

4. Brush the fish with olive oil and season with salt and pepper.

5. Bake for 8 to 10 minutes, or until the fish is just cooked through and flakes easily.

To Make a Flounder Pie

"Gut some flounders, wash them clean, dry them in a cloth, just boil them, cut off the meat clean, from the bones, lay a good crust over the dish and lay a little fresh butter in the bottom, and on that the fish; season with salt and pepper to your mind. Boil the bones in the water your fish was boiled in, with a little bit of horse-raddish, a little parsley, a very little bit of lemon-peel and a crust of bread. Boil it till there is just enough liquor for the pie then strain it, and put it in your pie; put on the top-crust and bake it."

—*The Art of Cookery Made Plain and Easy,* "Excelling any Thing of the Kind ever yet published," by Mrs. Glasse (1776)

Flounder Bonne Femme

This is one of the classic French preparations of sole. I made this dish for my then-husband-to-be on one of our first dates, using a Julia Child recipe. Maybe I was subconsciously trying to tell him I was indeed a *bonne femme*—or maybe it's just that I like mushrooms and flounder so much. Anyway, here's my little twist on the classic, using a variety of mushrooms and herbs.

SERVES 6.

4 tablespoons butter, divided

2 tablespoons finely chopped shallots

1 pound mixed mushrooms (porcini, oyster, shiitake, cremini, or a mixture of your favorites)

3 pounds flounder fillets

1½ cups dry white wine

1 tablespoon fresh lemon juice

1 tablespoon chopped parsley

1 tablespoon chopped fresh summer savory, tarragon, or your favorite herbs

1 teaspoon salt

¼ teaspoon white pepper

1½ tablespoons flour

1 cup heavy cream

Salt and pepper, to taste

1. Heat 2 tablespoons of the butter in a sauté pan. Add the shallots and mushrooms and cook until they begin to soften.

2. Fold the fillets into thirds and place in the pan. Add wine to just cover the fillets. Add the lemon juice, parsley, fresh herbs, salt, and pepper.

3. Cover the pan with a circle of waxed paper with a small vent hole cut in the middle. Bring to a boil. Reduce the heat and simmer for 3 minutes. Remove the fillets to a platter and keep them warm; leave the wine-mushroom mixture in the pan.

4. Blend the flour and 1 tablespoon of the butter into a paste.

5. Turn up the heat under the pan and reduce the wine-mushroom mixture by half. Add the flour-butter paste, whisking until thick and smooth. Add the cream, bring to a boil, and remove from the heat. Season to taste with salt and pepper.

6. Add the remaining butter a little at a time, shaking the pan gently to gradually melt it. Pour over the fish and glaze under a broiler until golden. Serve immediately.

Pan-Fried Flounder with Brown Sage Butter

Brown butter with sage is a classic Italian "sauce" for pasta—often ravioli or other pasta stuffed with squash or pumpkin—that is simple and elegant and lets the flavors of the dish shine through. That's why I like this so much over flounder. Oven-roasted winter squash would make a nice side dish.

SERVES 2–4.

½ cup flour

1 teaspoon sea salt

½ teaspoon white pepper

2 tablespoons butter, divided

1 tablespoon olive oil

½ cup fresh sage leaves, washed and dried

1 clove garlic, minced

1 pound flounder fillets

⅓ cup white wine

1. Combine the flour, salt, and pepper on a plate.

2. Heat 1 tablespoon of the butter, along with the oil, in a large sauté pan. Add the sage leaves and fry until crisp. Remove from the pan and drain on paper towels.

3. Add the garlic to the pan and sauté for 1 minute over medium heat.

4. Dredge the flounder fillets in the flour mixture and add to the pan. Sauté for 1 to 2 minutes over medium-high heat, or until golden brown on each side. Remove the fillets and keep them warm. Add the remaining butter and cook until just slightly colored. Add the wine to the pan and cook for 1 minute more.

5. Serve the fillets drizzled with pan juices, with the sage leaves crumbled over the top.

Haddock

"Give me a platter of choice finnan haddie, freshly cooked in its bath of water and milk, add melted butter, a slice or two of hot toast, a pot of steaming Darjeeling tea, and you may tell the butler to dispense with the caviar, truffles, and nightingales' tongues."

—Craig Claiborne

Biologically speaking, haddock is a part of the cod family, as are pollock, hake, tomcod, and other species noted in the Cod chapter. But for culinary purposes, haddock is such a delicious and popular fish that I decided to give it its own recipe section.

Haddock is now one of America's favorite fish, found in a vast number of New England restaurants from the humblest fried-food joint to top-notch restaurants. In the eighteenth and nineteenth centuries, however, haddock was considered only a poor relation of cod—primarily because it wasn't as good a salted fish. Fresh haddock was recognized for its wonderful flavor and texture, but was a smaller fishery. In the latter half of the nineteenth century, as fresh fish grew more popular than salted, haddock began to be fully appreciated. As its following grew, it became available smoked as finnan haddie, a popular food with the English and Scots immigrants in the Canadian maritime provinces, since finnan haddie is a much-loved British dish. The other factor was that haddock were,

and are, best caught on a line. Haddock caught in the nets used to catch cod just didn't hold up as well.

The good news is that haddock has finally earned its due respect as a foodstuff. There was a decline in the haddock fishery in the 1970s and '80s, but the stocks have made something of a comeback. The unpredictable catch from year to year is a factor in the survival of young haddock, which are also very popular dining choices for their cousins, cod and pollock. Not only that, but according to the Massachusetts Division of Marine Fisheries, "The number of larvae that survive in a given year is often chiefly determined by their location when they are ready to become bottom dwellers. If the currents in which they have been suspended have carried them far offshore from the continental shelf, few larvae will survive. Haddock populations characteristically suffer through extended series of years when few fish survive early life stages."

Haddock range all the way across the Atlantic, from the American side to the European. In summer they range from the southern part of the Grand Banks to Cape Cod. In the colder months, they can be found as far south as Cape Hatteras, North Carolina. You can tell a haddock from other members of the cod family by its three dorsal fins and a long black stripe running the length of the fish. The upper part of the fish is a violet-gray shade, gradually fading to a white underbelly. Again, consider using relatives like cusk, hake, and pollock.

Oven-"Fried" Fish-and-Chips

I love fish-and-chips, but my waistline does not. This is a lighter version based on a method of cooking fish developed by Mrs. Evalene Spencer of the U.S. Bureau of Fisheries in 1934, according to the *Encyclopedia of Fish Cookery*. You'll need a good hot oven—the temperature should get up to 500°F.

SERVES 6.

    1 tablespoon fine sea salt

    1 cup milk

    Finely sifted Italian-flavored bread crumbs

    2 teaspoons paprika, divided

    2 pounds haddock fillets, cut into 6 pieces

    6 medium russet potatoes, cut lengthwise into eighths and patted dry

    Nonstick cooking spray

    1 tablespoon coarse sea salt

1. Preheat the oven to 500°F. Grease a baking dish with vegetable oil.

2. In a bowl, stir the fine salt into the milk until dissolved. Place this to the left of your work area.

3. Combine the crumbs and 1 teaspoon of the paprika on a plate or in a shallow bowl. Place this to the right of your work area.

4. Using one hand to dip the fish into the salted milk, and the other hand for the dry ingredients, dip each piece of haddock into the milk and then roll it gently in the crumbs with your dry hand. Place on a baking dish.

5. Add the potatoes to the baking dish. Spray everything generously with nonstick spray. Sprinkle the coarse salt and remaining paprika on the potatoes and bake for 10 minutes. Serve hot with lemon wedges and tartar sauce (see the sidebar recipe, next page) if you like.

Tartar Sauce

This classic sauce for seafood has evolved over the years. The *1896 Boston Cooking School Cookbook* called for vinegar, lemon juice, Worcestershire sauce, and butter. By 1939 Imogene Wolcott's *New England Yankee Cookbook* offered a recipe similar to the one below. In keeping with trying to cut down on the fat and calories, I like to lighten up tartar sauce using reduced-fat mayonnaise.

1 cup reduced-fat mayonnaise
1 tablespoon minced onion
2 tablespoons sweet pickle relish
1 tablespoon fresh lemon juice
Pinch of Old Bay Seasoning
Salt and pepper, to taste

Combine all the ingredients in a bowl and refrigerate for at least an hour before using. This is great with any fried or oven-"fried" fish.

Smoky Haddock Chowder

Finnan haddie gives this chowder a wonderful smoky flavor. You could also add a bit of finnan haddie to the recipe for Salt Cod Cakes with Chili-Lime Mayonnaise on page 93 to give them a similar appeal.

SERVES 6.

> 1 slice thick-cut bacon, or 1 tablespoon diced salt pork
>
> ¼ pound finnan haddie or smoked haddock
>
> 1 large onion, chopped
>
> 5 medium potatoes, cut into ½-inch chunks
>
> 2 cups fish stock or water
>
> 1¼ pounds cod or haddock, cut into 1-inch pieces
>
> 1 pint (2 cups) light cream
>
> 1 (12-ounce) can evaporated skim milk
>
> Salt and pepper, to taste

1. In a frying pan, cook the bacon or salt pork until it's brown and the fat is rendered. Pour off all but 1 tablespoon of the fat.

2. Add the finnan haddie or smoked haddock, onion, and potatoes to the pan, and cook in the bacon fat until the onion is translucent. Add fish stock or water to cover, and simmer for 10 minutes. Flake the finnan haddie with a fork.

3. Add the cod or haddock, and simmer for another 5 to 10 minutes, or until the fish is cooked through. Separate the fish into pieces.

4. Add the cream and evaporated milk and heat through. Season to taste. Serve very hot with a dab of butter added to each bowl, if desired.

Baked Haddock with Crumb Topping

Baked haddock is probably the most common fish preparation in New England restaurants. It's nothing fancy and really easy to make, but baking it really lets the flavors of a great piece of haddock shine through.

SERVES 6.

> 1 cup dry stuffing mix, such as Pepperidge Farm Herb Seasoned Stuffing mix
> Juice of 1 lemon
> 4 tablespoons melted butter
> Salt and pepper, to taste
> 2 pounds haddock fillets, cut into 6 pieces

1. Preheat the oven to 450°F.

2. Combine the stuffing mix, lemon juice, and melted butter.

3. Salt and pepper the fillets to taste, and press equal amounts of topping onto each.

4. Bake for 10 minutes, or until the fish flakes easily and the topping is crisp and brown.

Halibut

Halibut seem to have inspired many legends over the years, possibly because among the flatfish—which include flounder, sole, plaice, and turbot—they are by far the largest.

Pre-Christian Norwegians regarded the halibut as a godlike fish, serious and wise. To this day the species is associated with feast days in Norway. In the New World, many of the halibut legends concern its size and vast appetite. Atlantic halibut (slightly different from the Pacific halibut) grow to about 700 pounds and as much as 9 feet long, although these specimens are becoming harder to come by. Most of the halibut caught these days are 50 to 100 pounds.

Captain John Smith, the seventeenth-century explorer, never shy about extolling the virtues of New England, wrote, "There is a large sized fish called the Hallibut, or Turbot: some are taken so bigg that that two men have much a doe to hall them into the boate: but there is such a plenty, that the fishermen onlye eat the heads & finnes, and throw away the bodies."

By the nineteenth century, inshore halibut stocks were diminishing. In 1876, it was a newsworthy event when some Noank, Connecticut, fishermen caught a few halibut about 8 miles from Mystic.

Offshore, large halibut were still being taken, and fishermen and naturalists seemed to delight in the astounding contents of their stomachs: live lobsters, a block of wood "a cubic foot in dimensions," an accordion key, pieces of iron, and "a large piece of floe ice."

In the *Fisheries and Fishery Industry of the United States, 1884*, Captain Collins, a halibut fisherman out of Gloucester, Massachusetts, documented (or at least claimed to have witnessed) some truly bizarre halibut behavior.

> *"The man at the wheel sang out that he saw a Halibut flapping its tale [sic] about a quarter of a mile off our starboard quarter. I looked through the spy-glass, and his statement was soon verified by the second appearance of the tail. We hove out a dory, and two men went in her, taking with them a pair of gaff-hooks. They soon returned bringing with them not only the Halibut, which was a fine one, of about seventy pounds' weight, but a small codfish which it had been trying to kill by striking it with its tail. The codfish was quite exhausted by the repeated blows, and did not attempt to escape after its enemy had been captured. The Halibut was so completely engaged in pursuit of the codfish that it paid no attention to the dory, and was easily captured."*

Throughout the twentieth century, the halibut catch continued to decline, although it has recovered somewhat in recent years. Most halibut purchased in the United States come from Canada and have been caught on deep-water longlines, baited hooks that lie on the seafloor. Halibut are being farmed in Norway, Canada, Scotland, and Iceland.

Chicken halibut (smaller and younger) are preferred because whale halibut can be firmer and drier. The flesh is white and delicately flavored. You may be able to find the highly prized halibut cheeks in some gourmet fish markets.

But unfortunately at least for now, halibut is on the watch list for decreased stocks. Since U.S. and Canadian line and harpooned swordfish are good—a sustainable choice according to the Monterey Bay Seafood Watch—you could substitute swordfish for any of these halibut recipes.

Ceviche

"If you get tired of the whole thing, you can slice almost any fine-grained fish in thin pieces, cover them with lemon or lime juice, and find them cooked in four hours without aid of stove or fire."

—M. F. K. Fisher, *How to Cook a Wolf*

Ceviche is a popular means of "cooking" fish without heat, using citrus and other seasoning. It originated in South America and can be used with a wide variety of fish and shellfish. Shrimp and scallops are particularly delicious. I sampled a version in Key West that included conch. Carleton Mitchell, sailor, adventurer, writer, and longtime friend of Mystic Seaport, writes about an exotic version of ceviche—or what he calls *poisson cru*—in his memoir *The Winds Call* about his adventures at sea:

Poisson cru—called *e i'a ota* in Tahitian, plain "raw fish" in English—had become my favorite Polynesian dish. Nothing is more delicious. Nor is it raw, except in the sense it is not cooked by heat. Now at last I was to see it made, as Terri took over the string Sam lifted aboard.

Almost any sort of fish may be used, although Tahitians consider bonito best. After cleaning, scaling and dicing into small cubes, it was put in a bowl, and the juice of perhaps a dozen limes squeezed over—enough to thoroughly dampen the flesh. Terri anointed a layer, salted it generously and turned it with a fork, making sure none was missed. Onions were sliced in, and given a thorough tossing to mix. The bowl was covered to marinate. Thirty minutes is sufficient to cook to the taste of a true convert. After an hour the meat is done enough for almost anyone. It has the taste and texture of cooked fish, and the flavor is not strong. Excess juice is drained off and salad ingredients added—sliced tomatoes, more chopped onions, diced carrot, halved hard-boiled egg, lettuce—none or all as fancy dictates. Ideally, milk from pressed coconut meat should be poured over just before serving, but this is not essential.

Oil-Poached Halibut
with Sun-Dried Tomato Coulis

You would think that poaching in oil would result in a greasy fish, but the result is actually a buttery tenderness that melts in your mouth.

SERVE 4–6.

> 3 cups olive oil
>
> ⅓ cup white truffle oil
>
> 1 head garlic
>
> 1½ pounds halibut fillets or steaks
>
> 1 cup sun-dried tomatoes in oil
>
> 1 tablespoon balsamic vinegar
>
> 1 teaspoon sea salt
>
> ⅓ cup fish or chicken stock
>
> Salt and pepper, to taste

1. In a deep pan large enough to hold all the fish without crowding, combine the oils and begin to warm them over low heat.

2. Separate the cloves of garlic from the head, and rub off any loose, papery skin—but do not peel. Add the garlic cloves to the oil.

3. Slowly bring the oil up to about 170°F, letting the garlic cook in it; this should take about 10 minutes.

4. Add the halibut and poach for 10 to 12 minutes, keeping the oil at about 170°F. When the fish is just cooked through and flakes nicely, remove the garlic and halibut from the oil. Keep the halibut warm.

5. Peel the garlic cloves and add them to a food processor. Add the sun-dried tomatoes, vinegar, sea salt, ¼ cup of the poaching oil, and the stock. Process to a sauce consistency.

6. Season the fish with salt and pepper, and serve with the sun-dried tomato sauce.

Grilled Halibut with Nectarine-Poblano Salsa

I love to grill fish any time of year, but when fish is fresh and plentiful in summer, it makes for a wonderful, simple warm-weather meal. If you hit it just right, you'll be able to get seriously fresh nectarines, or you can substitute peeled peaches. Since halibut is not always a good sustainable choice, consider mako or line-caught swordfish.

SERVES 4–6.

1 ripe but firm nectarine, seeded and chopped

2 medium ripe tomatoes, seeded and chopped

½ red bell pepper, finely chopped

½ red onion, finely chopped

½ poblano pepper, minced

Juice of 1 lime

2 teaspoons soy sauce

1 tablespoon rice wine vinegar

3 tablespoons extra-virgin olive oil, divided

1½ pounds halibut steaks

Sea salt and fresh pepper, to taste

1. Preheat a gas grill, or light the charcoal.

2. In a nonreactive bowl, combine all the ingredients except 1 tablespoon of the olive oil, the halibut, and the salt and pepper. Cover and refrigerate, letting the salsa sit for at least 1 hour or up to 4.

3. Brush the halibut steaks with the remaining olive oil, and season with salt and pepper. Grill over high heat for 4 to 5 minutes on each side, or until the fish is opaque and flaky. Serve with the salsa on the side.

Mackerel

"Mackerel scales and mare's tails make lofty ships carry low sails." This sailor's weather adage refers to the clouds that resemble the scales that run down the sides of the Atlantic mackerel and the plume-like clouds that look like horse's tails. They portend strong winds.

This plentiful fish was once a mainstay of New England commercial fishing, and while there is still a commercial mackerel fishery, using chiefly purse seines and trawls, the species' popularity has been somewhat eclipsed. Mackerel are a common catch for recreational fishermen, as they are found near shore in the summer months and are easily caught with rod and reel. Mackerel travel in schools and appear in Atlantic coastal waters in spring. They average about a pound but can run up to 2 pounds. Unlike more overfished species, there are few, if any, restrictions for anglers.

Before 1870, virtually all the mackerel that were caught were salted aboard ship and often referred to as "Boston mackerel." Salting made sense. Being an oily fish, mackerel spoils easily. In the days before icing or canning was possible, the catch would not have

made it to the table before developing an off-taste. This short shelf life has given mackerel a bad rap, in my view, as fresh-caught mackerel cooked over hot coals are a real summer treat. There was a boom in mackerel fishing in the late 1800s, but the fishery—and demand—has come and gone cyclically ever since.

Canned mackerel in tomato sauce is still popular in the United Kingdom and Scandinavia, and mackerel is a fairly common ingredient in sushi. Mackerel is full of healthy oils and is considered safer for regular consumption than some of the more popular food fish, such as tuna and halibut, and vastly more sustainable.

When I was a kid, one of our neighbors would take his aluminum skiff out into the cove in front of our house as often as possible and bring home mackerel by the bucketful. Everyone for miles around had their freezers filled with cleaned and gutted mackerel. And though it is a tasty fish, there can be too much of a good thing. The local barn cats and herring gulls often had a feast when it came time to clean out the fridge at the end of the summer.

> *"To broil mackerel—clean and split them open; wipe dry; lay them on a clean gridiron, rubbed with suet, over a very clear slow fire; turn; season with pepper, salt and a little butter; fine minced parsley is also used."*
>
> —*Early American Cookery: The Good Housekeeper*
> by Sarah Josepha Hale (1841)

Smoked Mackerel Pâté

This flavorful spread is based on Ducktrap River Fish Farms' smoked mackerel. Ducktrap was founded in 1978 in Lincolnville, Maine, as a two-person trout-farming operation. After battling marauding raccoons, otters, skunks, and owls, which seemed to want the trout as much as they did, the owners built a 4-by-4-foot smokehouse with an old woodstove and tried their hand at smoking seafood. They now have more than 145 employees and produce more than thirty-five smoked products, using all-natural ingredients, native hardwoods and fruit woods, and ecofriendly methods. This recipe is adapted from their cookbook, available from www.ducktrap.com.

Serve this tasty Mediterranean spread on crisp toast or lightly toasted French bread.

SERVES A CROWD!

½ pound brine-cured Greek, French, or Italian black olives, pitted

8 ounces Ducktrap River smoked mackerel

½ cup drained capers

1 small clove garlic, chopped

½ cup extra-virgin olive oil

2 tablespoons Metaxa or brandy

¼ bunch Italian parsley

1. Combine all the ingredients in a food processor and pulse very briefly, just until a coarse spread forms. (The tapenade can be prepared up to 1 week ahead. Pack it in a container, pour a thin layer of olive oil on top, and refrigerate. Bring to room temperature and stir before serving.)

2. Serve with crusty bread or crackers and lemon slices.

Grilled Mackerel with Citrus and Fennel

SERVES 4.

½ teaspoon grated fresh orange zest

½ teaspoon finely grated fresh lemon zest

1½ tablespoons fresh lemon juice

Salt and pepper, to taste

⅓ cup extra-virgin olive oil

3 tablespoons finely chopped fresh oregano, plus 4 large sprigs

4 (1-pound) whole Atlantic mackerel

2 tablespoons vegetable oil

8 (¼-inch-thick) lemon slices

1 bulb fennel, sliced

¼ cup chopped flat-leaf parsley

1. Light a charcoal grill or preheat a gas grill.

2. Whisk the orange and lemon zests with the lemon juice, salt, pepper, and olive oil; whisk until combined well. Whisk in the chopped oregano. Measure out ¼ cup of this mixture to brush on the fish while grilling.

3. Gut the fish and remove their heads. Score the mackerel vertically at 2-inch intervals on both sides, then brush them all over with the vegetable oil and season generously with salt and pepper. Season each cavity with salt and pepper, then place 2 lemon slices, a quarter of the fennel slices, and an oregano sprig inside and close with skewers. If the lemon slices are too large to fit in the cavity, cut them in half horizontally.

4. Spray the grill rack with nonstick cooking spray, and cook the mackerel for 5 to 7 minutes, depending on their size. Turn them over and continue grilling until they're just cooked through and flaky, about 3 to 5 minutes more. Remove them carefully from the grill using a spatula and tongs. Drizzle the remaining lemon-oil mixture over each fish, sprinkle with the parsley, and serve.

Salmon

When Pliny the Elder wrote nearly 2,000 years ago that "In Aquatania the Salmon surpasseth all the fishes of the sea," this wasn't news. Since prehistoric times, salmon have been appreciated, even revered. Salmon figure prominently in Native American legends, and their remains have been found at burial sites dating as far back as 25,000 years.

A life-size salmon carved on the overhang of Abri du Poisson in the Gorge d'Enfer in France may be as much as 35,000 years old. No one looking at that beautiful carving can doubt that the person who carved it had a special reverence for this fish.

Unlike many other kinds of native fish, the early settlers knew about salmon. It was highly valued in Britain and became much in demand in New England. In the eighteenth century, salmon were caught in great numbers in the larger rivers in New England—the Connecticut and the Penobscot were two of the most abundant sources.

Unlike West Coast salmon, not all of the Atlantic fish die after spawning; some return to the sea. The young salmon stay in rivers and estuaries for about three years before leaving for salt water.

We think of depleted fisheries as a fairly recent phenomenon, but in fact the Atlantic salmon fishery was one of the very first to be wiped out by industrial activity in New

England. Overfishing, the damming of rivers, and the release of effluents into waterways all took an early toll on such species as the salmon and shad that travel upriver to spawn. The salmon population of the Connecticut River was virtually gone by the mid-1800s. Salmon survived in the Merrimac till later in the century and made their last stand on the Down East coast of Maine, where most of the catch was iced and shipped to Boston for sale.

By this time, line fishing for salmon had long since given way to stationary nets. In Maine, the small, open Lincolnville wherry was designed for inshore use to set the salmon nets and to retrieve the catch. The last New England fish house and equipment—which belonged to Robie Ames of Northport, Maine—are now on display at Mystic Seaport Museum after seeing their last use in the 1940s, when the fish became so scarce that even a single family could not make a living from them. About this time canned Pacific Northwest salmon became popular, further reducing demand for Atlantic salmon.

According to an interview with Robie Ames preserved in the museum's archives, he did not catch any salmon less than 8 pounds; fish any smaller slipped through nets. Salmon ran up to 16 or 18 pounds, and averaged 10 to 12. The first salmon of the season were shipped to Faneuil Hall market in Boston.

Thankfully, careful husbandry, research, and conservation efforts, as well as restocking using Atlantic salmon from Maine and Canada, have taken the fish off the endangered species list (although, ironically, some stocks of the remaining salmon in Maine are considered endangered). Salmon are particularly amenable to aquaculture, and farmed fish are now readily available year-round. Norway and Chile are world leaders in farmed salmon, but Maine also has substantial salmon farms.

The wild salmon population is still struggling to some degree, but the Connecticut and Penobscot Rivers now have returning populations.

There's good reason for salmon's ageless popularity. The flesh is firm and attractively pink-orange, while the flavor is pronounced but not too fishy. They are particularly versatile: Salmon can be planked, grilled, baked, smoked, dried, or canned. They are high in vitamins A and B and omega-3 oils.

> *"As food, fish is easier of digestion than meats are, with the exception of salmon; this kind of fish is extremely hearty food, and should be given sparingly to children, and used cautiously by those who have weak stomachs, or who take little exercise."*
>
> —*Early American Cookery: The Good Housekeeper*
> by Sarah Josepha Hale (1841)

Salmon with Tri-Pepper Salsa

The *J. & E. Riggin*—part of the Maine windjammer fleet—is known for her excellent food. She was built in 1927 in Dorchester, New Jersey, as an oystering schooner and won the only oystering schooner race in 1929. Today, owners Anne Mahle, food columnist, cookbook author, and one of the finest schooner cooks in the fleet, and her husband, Captain Jon Finger, serve their guests delicious dishes like this one, which appears in *At Home, At Sea: Recipes from the Maine Windjammer* J.&E. Riggin.

SERVES 4–6.

Tri-Pepper Salsa

½ red bell pepper, seeded, julienned, and cut into 1-inch pieces

½ green bell pepper, seeded, julienned, and cut into 1-inch pieces

½ yellow bell pepper, seeded, julienned, and cut into 1-inch pieces

1 red onion, cut in half and thinly sliced

3 tablespoons extra-virgin olive oil

Juice of 1½ limes

2 tablespoons chopped fresh dill

½ teaspoon salt

Freshly ground pepper, to taste

Salmon

4–6 (6-ounce) salmon fillets

¼ cup fresh lemon juice

¼ cup extra-virgin olive oil

¼ cup white wine

1 teaspoon salt

Freshly ground black pepper

1. To make the salsa, toss the vegetables with the olive oil, lime juice, and dill.

2. Add salt and pepper to taste.

3. Allow the mixture to sit at room temperature for an hour (2 at the most—you don't want it to get soggy). Check the seasonings before serving.

4. Preheat the oven to 375°F.

5. Place the salmon fillets in a nonreactive 9 x 13-inch baking dish. Drizzle the fish with the lemon juice, olive oil, and white wine, and season with salt and pepper. Let sit for 15 minutes to marinate.

6. Bake, uncovered, for 15 to 20 minutes. Remove the fish when it's still slightly darker in the center. It will continue to cook when you take it out of the oven.

7. Serve immediately topped with the Tri-Pepper Salsa.

Miso-Soy Glazed Salmon

Today we know salmon to be one of the healthiest foods around—full of omega-3 fatty acids but low in calories and high in protein.

SERVES 4-6.

> 1 cup soy sauce
>
> ⅓ cup miso paste
>
> 1 tablespoon toasted sesame oil
>
> 2 tablespoons brown sugar
>
> ¼ cup peanut oil
>
> 1 teaspoon chili-garlic sauce
>
> 1 shallot, minced
>
> 1 (2-pound) salmon fillet

1. Preheat the oven to 425°F.

2. Combine all ingredients except the salmon in a bowl. Refrigerate until ready to use.

3. Place the salmon on a baking sheet or glass baking dish, and brush it generously with the glaze. Bake for 20 minutes, or until it's opaque and just cooked through and the glaze has browned and caramelized.

Smoked and Cured Fish

Salmon is perhaps the most commonly smoked and cured fish in the world. Smoked salmon is a real delicacy and is now readily available in grocery stores and fish markets. It makes a wonderful and elegant hors d'oeuvre served on slices of cocktail rye with some mustard, finely chopped red onion, and a sprig of dill.

There are two methods of smoking salmon or any fish, for that matter: hot smoking and cold smoking. First, the fish are salted or brined and kept cool. Hot-smoked salmon is cooked at a higher temperature, generally between 120°F and 180°F. The temperature is gradually increased over a period of six to eight hours. In cold smoking, the fish is not actually cooked but cured in smoke with temperatures between 70°F and 90°F for a longer period. The texture of cold-smoked salmon is more like gravlax or lox. Hot-smoked salmon has a texture more like cooked fish.

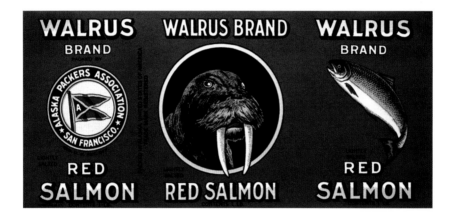

Gravlax

Gravlax is a traditional Scandinavian method of curing fish in a blend of salt, sugar, and dill. Although purists reject the idea, I have experimented with adding juniper berries, tarragon, aquavit, or even citrus vodka—with excellent results.

SERVES 8 AS AN APPETIZER.

½ **cup kosher salt**

½ **cup sugar**

2 tablespoons cracked white peppercorns

2 teaspoons juniper berries

1 (1-pound) fresh salmon fillet, skin on

1 large bunch fresh dill, stems included

1. Mix the salt, sugar, white peppercorns, and juniper berries.

2. Rub a handful of this mixture on both sides of the salmon. Place the salmon in a glass or other nonreactive dish, and sprinkle the rest of the mix on top.

3. Cover the salmon with dill, wrap it in plastic wrap, and return to the dish. Refrigerate for 48 hours, depending on how thick the salmon is and how salty you'd like it.

4. Slice the salmon off the skin and slice into thin slivers. Serve with your favorite mustard sauce.

Salmon and Leek Pie with a Puff Pastry Crust

This dish harkens back to English pub menus, as in going out "for a pie and a pint." Denise Landis, former *New York Times* recipe tester and publisher of The Cook's Cook (www.thecookscook.com), developed this dish. It makes a lovely addition to a potluck or picnic.

SERVES 4–6.

8 tablespoons (1 stick) butter

4 leeks, white and light green parts only, halved lengthwise, rinsed, and sliced ¼ inch thick

2 large carrots, peeled and chopped into ½-inch pieces

Salt, to taste

2 garlic cloves

½ cup all-purpose flour

1 cup milk

1 (8-ounce) bottle clam juice

2 pounds skinless, boneless salmon fillets, cut into 1-inch pieces

1¼ cups frozen peas

Pinch of freshly grated nutmeg

⅓ cup minced fresh dill

2 tablespoons fresh lemon juice

Ground white pepper, to taste

1 (9½ x 9-inch) sheet frozen puff pastry, thawed

1 egg, lightly beaten

1. Preheat oven to 400°F. Place a large skillet over medium heat, and add butter. When the butter has melted, add leeks, carrots, and salt to taste. Stir until leeks are soft, 5 to 7 minutes. Stir in garlic with a wooden spoon. Reduce heat to medium-low, add flour, and stir constantly until pale golden yellow, about 3 minutes. Add milk and clam juice, whisking constantly, and simmer until the sauce is thickened and smooth. Remove from heat.

2. Place salmon in a large heatproof mixing bowl. Add hot leek mixture and sauce, and stir well. Add frozen peas, nutmeg, dill, and lemon juice. Season with salt and pepper to taste. Transfer mixture to a 9- or 10-inch deep-dish pie plate, and set aside.

3. Dust a work surface with flour and unfold the sheet of puff pastry. Roll pastry out so it is large enough to cut a disk that will completely cover the pie, 11 to 12 inches. Brush the edge of the pastry lightly with beaten egg, and drape the crust over the pie, pressing on the edge to seal it to the pie plate. Brush the surface of the dough with the remaining egg.

4. Bake the pie until the top is puffed and golden brown, about 15 minutes. If the pastry seems to be browning too quickly, drape lightly with a sheet of foil. Allow the pie to sit at room temperature for about 5 minutes before serving.

Smoked Salmon Frittata

A frittata is a sort of crustless quiche that may combine all manner of meats, veggies, fish, or herbs and is finished under the broiler. Frittatas are standard on Spanish tapas menus. This makes a lovely brunch or supper dish or even an appetizer. There are endless varieties, but this one balances the smoky flavor of the salmon with herbs and vegetables.

SERVES 6.

2 tablespoons butter

1 leek, white part only, thinly sliced

1 cup sliced wild mushrooms, such as porcini or shiitake

1 shallot, chopped

8 eggs

⅓ cup light cream

4 ounces smoked salmon, flaked or cut into ½-inch pieces

2 tablespoons chopped fresh chives

2 tablespoons chopped fresh parsley

Salt and pepper, to taste

1 tablespoon olive oil

1. Heat the butter in a small sauté pan over medium heat. Add the leek, mushrooms, and shallot, and sauté for 4 to 5 minutes, stirring occasionally. Set aside to cool.

2. Lightly beat the eggs with the cream in a large bowl. Stir in the smoked salmon, mushroom mixture, and herbs. Season with salt and pepper.

3. Heat the olive oil in a 10-inch nonstick skillet over medium heat; pour in the egg mixture. As the eggs start to cook, pull in the cooked edges with a spatula to allow the uncooked egg on top to move to the bottom of the pan for even cooking. When the frittata is almost set (firm but still somewhat liquid on top), place the pan under the broiler to finish cooking the top. Slide the frittata onto a cutting board and cut into wedges. Serve hot or at room temperature.

Shad and Shad Roe

Massachusetts has its Sacred Cod, but the state of Connecticut has its shad. Although only designated as the state fish in 2003, shad was an important food source long before the first white settlers landed on New England shores. Native Americans saw shad as a seasonal gift and were known to have large springtime gatherings to roast these fish over open wood fires, often planking them (much the way salmon is prepared in the Pacific Northwest). The technique is used to this day in springtime Connecticut shad bakes.

Typically, among the early settlers, food that was in an overabundant supply and consumed by the Natives was viewed with skepticism. Like lobster and other bounties of the sea, in the early colonial days, shad was considered poor people's food—fed to servants and used as fertilizer. Thousands of barrels of shad were shipped off to Revolutionary War troops and reputedly staved off hunger in some very lean times.

The fish themselves spend most of their lives in the ocean but begin to make their way up freshwater rivers in spring, when it comes time to spawn. Indeed, the return of the shad is such a reliable harbinger of springtime that the shadbush and the shad frog—both of which flourish in early spring—take their names from the species' return. Shad begin to appear in rivers of the Northeast as early as March; they show their faces in the Connecticut River between April and June. By summer, the shad are headed back to sea.

Shad is a member of the herring family and is valued not only for its flavorful meat, but also for its excellent roe. The biggest drawback to enjoying shad is the number of bones—some 1,300 in an adult fish, which grow to roughly 30 inches and typically weigh in at 3 to 5 pounds. And to make things even more challenging, the bones do not follow a neat pattern as they do in other bony fish; they run both horizontally and vertically. Old-time shad boners guarded their techniques carefully, and for most of us, buying boneless fillets—or getting invited to a Connecticut shad bake—is the best bet.

New Potatoes with Caviar and Crème Fraîche

You can buy crème fraîche in the supermarket, but making your own is simple. Combine 3 parts heavy cream and 2 parts yogurt or buttermilk in a glass bowl. Cover and let stand at room temperature for 12 hours, until thick and creamy.

SERVES 12 AS AN HORS D'OEUVRE.

> 12 small red new potatoes
>
> ¼ cup olive oil
>
> Black pepper, to taste
>
> ½ cup crème fraîche
>
> 1 small jar lumpfish caviar (Be guided by your tastes and your budget!)
>
> Fresh dill sprigs, for garnish

1. Preheat the oven to 350°F.

2. Rub the potatoes all over with the olive oil. Sprinkle with black pepper.

3. Bake the potatoes for 35 minutes, or until just soft. Halve the potatoes and scoop out the insides, leaving the skins for a shell.

4. Mash the potato flesh with the crème fraîche, and spoon back into the shells. Top with caviar and a sprig of dill.

Roes by Any Other Name . . .

"One can be unhappy before eating caviar, even after, but at least not during."

—Alexander Korda

Caviar is, of course, the queen of fish roe. It is the eggs of sturgeons, those prehistoric armored bottom feeders. The highest-quality caviar, like wildly expensive beluga, sevruga, and osetra, came historically from the Caspian or Black Sea.

But in the past thirty years, the stock of sturgeon in the Caspian has plunged to 10 percent of its previous total due to rampant overfishing. A United Nations ban on the export of most caviar (except Iranian) from the Caspian Sea has left true beluga caviar hard to find. Now other sources are taking up the slack, including American farm-raised caviar. Some experts predict that America will soon become a leading caviar producer once again.

Caviar is almost as famous for its astronomical prices as for its exquisite, briny flavor. But this wasn't always the case. If you went into a tavern in New York City in the early 1800s, you might well have been given a free supply of caviar so that its saltiness would encourage you to purchase more libations than you might have planned—much the way popcorn and salted nuts are served today in your neighborhood bar. In those days, the Hudson and Delaware Rivers teemed with massive sturgeon, and caviar became known as "Albany beef." But by the early 1910s, the fishery was virtually nonexistent—the usual culprits of overfishing and environmental destruction had once again taken their toll.

The term *caviar* should really apply only to sturgeon roe, but you can find it applied to all kinds of roe—bowfin, whitefish, salmon, and paddlefish. Inexpensive jars of lumpfish and salmon roe, available in most grocery stores, make good caviar substitutes; mix them with sour cream or cream cheese and a squeeze of lemon to make a nice appetizer. Topping deviled eggs with caviar is also a great way to spruce up standard party fare.

Shad roe usually comes in two roughly symmetrical lobes surrounded by a thin membrane. Each lobe is generally considered enough for one serving. The roe is often wrapped in bacon and pan-fried or broiled and served with lemon—or with scrambled eggs. Shad roe has a delicate flavor that bears little relation to the strong, briny taste of caviar.

Americans don't eat a lot of fish roes these days, but someone, somewhere eats just about every kind of roe: Herring, lumpfish, whitefish, flying fish, haddock, pollock, salmon, cod, lobster, tuna, urchin, and many more are all popular. The Japanese, Korean, and Scandinavian peoples may be the most enthusiastic roe consumers.

Connecticut Stuffed Baked Shad

This recipe is adapted from *The Yankee Cookbook*, published in 1939 and attributed to the "New England kitchen of Louise Crathern Russell."

SERVES 6.

> 1 large shad (about 5 pounds)
> 1 cup cracker crumbs
> 4 tablespoons melted butter
> ¼ teaspoon salt
> ¼ teaspoon pepper
> 1 small onion, minced
> 1 teaspoon sage
> 1 cup hot water
> ¼ pound sliced bacon

1. Preheat the oven to 400°F.

2. Make sure the fish has been cleaned and gutted, but leave its head and tail on. Rinse well and pat dry.

3. In a bowl, combine the cracker crumbs, butter, salt, pepper, onion, and sage. Stuff the cavity of the fish with this mixture and sew the edges together.

4. Place the fish on a rack in a baking pan. Add water to the pan. Lay the bacon slices over the shad.

5. Bake for 10 minutes at 400°F, then reduce the heat to 325°F and bake for another 30 minutes, basting frequently to keep the fish tender and well browned.

Broiled Shad Roe

This recipe is from *The Herald Tribune's Home Institute Cookbook*, a classic and best-selling American cookbook originally published in 1937.

SERVES 6.

> **3 pairs shad roe**
> **8 tablespoons butter, melted**
> **Salt and pepper, to taste**
> **Lemon wedges**

1. Preheat the oven to 400°F.

2. Brush the roe with the melted butter. Sprinkle with salt and pepper to taste, and broil for 5 minutes on each side.

3. Serve with Maître d'Hotel Butter (see the sidebar recipe).

Maître d'Hotel Butter

Maître d'Hotel Butter is one of the most classic additions to fish of all kinds. It's simple and elegant and brings out the best in fresh seafood. Store some in the refrigerator and use it on grilled or broiled fish.

> **8 tablespoons butter, room temperature**
> **1 tablespoon minced parsley**
> **1½ tablespoons fresh lemon juice**
> **½ teaspoon sea salt**
> **Dash of white pepper**

Cream the butter until soft. Add the remaining ingredients and beat until fluffy.

Sautéed Shad Roe with Applewood Bacon

Classic preparations for shad roe are generally pretty simple and often include bacon, which adds a nice salty, smoky touch.

SERVES 6.

2 strips apple-cured bacon

1 tablespoon butter

½ cup sliced shallots

¼ cup flour

½ teaspoon salt

Freshly ground pepper, to taste

3 pairs shad roe

Chopped chives, for garnish

Lemon wedges, for garnish

1. Cook the bacon in a large frying pan until crisp. Remove the bacon and drain it on paper towels. Add the butter to the frying pan and melt.

2. Add the shallots and sauté until soft.

3. Mix the flour, salt, and pepper on a plate. Dredge the shad roe in this seasoned flour, shaking off any excess.

4. Increase the heat to medium, and add the roe to the pan. Fry for about 5 minutes on each side, until golden brown.

5. Serve hot, with the pan juices poured over and garnished with crumbled bacon, chopped chives, and lemon wedges on the side.

Smelts

On both coasts and throughout the Great Lakes region, smelts have happy associations. Although they can be taken in winter from fish shacks on the ice, early spring is when the smelts run in the river mouths and are caught in great abundance with lines and nets. So after the long winter, when everybody's ready for a good party, a smelt fry is a coastal tradition. There are likely to be deep-fried smelts, sautéed smelts, baked smelts, smoked smelts—even pickled smelts.

Smelts are small fish, generally between 6 and 9 inches long and slender, with a bright silver skin. They're most often eaten whole, the crispy tail being a particular favorite, although some people prefer to remove the backbone (which pulls out easily from the cooked fish). The other bones are so soft that, other than adding a little texture, they are in no way unpleasant to eat.

The most common variety in the North Atlantic is the rainbow smelt. Although they have a high oil content, when fresh, these fish have a light flavor and a scent that some say resembles cucumbers. Certain West Coast smelts are called candlefish: Their oil content is so high that Native Alaskans once dried them, inserted a twig for a wick, and burned them like candles!

Smelts are members of the herring family, as are the shad and alewives that they closely resemble. They were an important food source through the nineteenth century.

Captain John Smith, that seventeenth-century explorer who promoted the wonders of New England back to his English homeland, claimed that fishermen here took twelve hogsheads (barrels) of alewives in one night. In the Massachusetts Fisheries Report of 1870, smelts were so plentiful in Boston's Back Bay that residents of "lower Beacon Street might be seen at early hours, eagerly catching their breakfast from their back door."

> *To Fry Smelts*
> *"Smelts should be very fresh, and not washed more than is necessary to clean them. Dry them in a cloth, lightly flour, dip them in egg, and sprinkle over with very fine breadcrumbs, and put them into boiling lard. Fry of a nice pale brown, and be careful not to take off the light roughness of the crumbs, or their beauty will be spoiled. Dry them before the fire on a drainer, and serve with plain melted butter. This fish is often used as a garnishing."*
> —Mrs. Beeton's Household Management (1861)

Fried Smelts

This is an Italian-influenced method of frying smelts.

SERVES 4–6.

1 cup Italian bread crumbs

½ cup freshly grated pecorino-Romano cheese

½ teaspoon sea salt

2 pounds smelts, dressed

2 eggs, lightly beaten

Vegetable oil for deep-frying

1. In a bowl, combine the bread crumbs, cheese, and salt.

2. Rinse the smelts and dry them thoroughly. Dip each piece into the beaten eggs, and then dredge in the bread crumb mixture.

3. Dry the fish on a cake rack for 15 minutes so the breading can set.

4. Meanwhile, heat the oil to 365°F. When it's hot, deep-fry the smelts until golden brown, about 4 minutes. Drain on paper towels, and serve with lemon wedges and tartar sauce.

Boquerones (Portuguese-Style Smelts)

Boquerones are Spanish tapas often made with anchovies marinated in vinegar. This delicious Portuguese-inspired dish is from Robert La Moia, who was the chef/owner of La Moia Tapas Bar & Café in Providence, Rhode Island. Corn flour is also known as masa flour or *masa harina* and can be found in the Hispanic foods section in most supermarkets.

SERVES 4–6.

½ cup corn flour
⅓ cup wheat flour
1 tablespoon salt
1 egg
¼ cup milk
¾ cup water
3 cups cornflakes

2 pounds smelts, dressed
Vegetable oil as needed for frying
2–3 tablespoons olive oil
1 tablespoon chopped garlic
½ teaspoon red pepper flakes
¼–½ cup sherry vinegar

1. Mix the corn and wheat flours with the salt. Beat in the egg and milk. Slowly add the water until the mixture resembles thin pancake batter.

2. Crush the cornflakes into small pieces, but don't pulverize them.

3. Wash and dry the smelts thoroughly. Dip them in the batter, then roll them in the cornflakes. You can proceed with cooking the smelts at this point, or refrigerate or even freeze them for later.

4. In a deep pot, heat the oil to 360°F. Drop the smelts into the hot oil a few at a time so as not to overcrowd them. Cook until golden brown. Remove the smelts from the oil and drain on paper towels.

5. Heat the olive oil in a frying pan. Add the garlic and red pepper and cook until sizzling, but don't let the garlic brown, as it will become bitter. Add the smelts to the pan and swirl to heat them.

6. Add the sherry vinegar and carefully ignite, allowing the flames to subside and the vinegar to evaporate. Serve the smelts immediately.

Squid

In New England, squid are mostly associated with Italian cuisine (calamari), but they are equally at home in Spanish and Portuguese dishes, including paella and squid in their ink. (As an aficionado of all things Portuguese, I would like to see squid become known by their Portuguese name *lula*—surely the prettiest of their names!)

Squid are cephalopods, like octopuses and cuttlefish, which means that they aren't fin fish—or fish at all, really. They're actually shellfish, but not bivalves or crustaceans. So what are they doing in the "Fin Fish" section? Well, with apologies to any marine biologist who might be reading this, I like them so much I had to include them *somewhere*. And here they are.

Cuttlefish are much like squid but have a cuttlebone used for buoyancy—familiar to us from its use in canary cages. A memorable meal in Cuenca, Spain, was sautéed small cuttlefish stuffed with their own tentacles and accompanied by a sauce of their black ink. Cuttlefish, rather than squid, are often used in this preparation as they have more ink. (This ink, called sepia, used to be a valuable dye.) Most cuttlefish are imported into this country, and since their taste is so close to that of squid, they may not be worth their higher price.

Squid themselves come in sizes from 1 inch to 60 feet. It's only in the past few years, however, that live giant squid have been captured—two of them, both about 25 feet long. One of these examples is preserved in a tank at the National Museum of London. Larger dead squid have been found, and of course *much* larger ones exist in terrifying legends—including the Scandinavian "Kraken" tale of a giant squid attacking and sinking ships. Legend held that the Kraken was as much as a mile in circumference.

Most of the squid for the table are hardly giant, however. With a body length of 2 inches or so, they are cooked whole. Larger ones are usually cut into rings after removing the skin, head, and small mantle. Expecting the usual plateful of 2-inchers, I was once taken aback to be served a single Portuguese *lula* of about 9 inches long. It was tender and mild.

Squid is caught both for the table and as bait. It may be the most versatile bait in the ocean—species ranging from flounder to stripers to swordfish will all go for squid. It takes to freezing well, so it can be preserved for future use. Alas, what it doesn't tolerate is overcooking—it turns as chewy as a rubber band.

In New England, commercial draggers catch most of the squid during April and May. Fishermen also jig for squid using specialized lures with two sets of multiple hooks. Squid are attracted to light, so some squidders shine bright lights into the water or fish near street lamps.

At the fish market, squid are sold already cleaned. If you're lucky enough to get some fresh ones, cleaning isn't difficult—but there is a knack to it. First remove the transparent quill under the mantle, then pull the head off; most of the guts will come with it. Pull off the skin, starting with one of the wings, and rinse. For more detailed instructions and tips, you can go to squidfish.net

Calamari Trizzano

This is a recipe from Angela Sanfilippo, who came to Gloucester from Sicily in 1965 and was president of the Gloucester Fishermen's Wives Association. This association of determined women played a vital role in protecting fishing grounds and went head-to-head with Big Oil when there was a proposal to drill for oil in Georges Bank. They have also been a major force in developing balanced management plans for creating sustainable fisheries, as well as improving safety conditions aboard fishing vessels. Not exactly a coffee klatch! The association's cookbook is a treasure.

SERVES 5–6.

⅓ cup olive oil

2 cups sliced onions

3 pounds cleaned calamari or squid, cut into rings

3 tablespoons pine nuts

3 tablespoons raisins

¼ cup fresh parsley

2 teaspoons salt

Black pepper, to taste

1 (28-ounce) can crushed tomatoes

1 pound spaghetti (optional)

1. Heat the olive oil in a skillet and sauté the onions. Add the calamari and sauté until golden.

2. Add the nuts, raisins, parsley, salt, pepper, and crushed tomatoes. Cook over medium heat for about 20 minutes. Remove from the heat and let the mixture sit for 15 minutes.

3. Serve in individual bowls with Italian bread. If you'd like to serve with spaghetti, cook the pasta according to package directions. Drain and mix with the calamari sauce. Sprinkle with Romano cheese. This dish can also be served with white rice.

Calamari Fritti

Fried calamari has become more and more popular, especially in coastal seafood restaurants. It's often served with a tartar sauce or marinara sauce for dipping and is just great with a glass of cold beer or Italian white wine. I make mine with masa harina or golden corn flour.

SERVES 6.

Oil for deep-frying

2 pounds small squid, cleaned

1 cup golden corn flour

1 teaspoon sea salt

½ teaspoon white pepper

2 teaspoons dried oregano

1 egg

1. In a deep pot, heat enough oil to easily accommodate the squid, bringing the temperature high enough so the calamari bubble briskly when you put them in.

2. Rinse and dry the squid thoroughly. Slice it into rings, leaving the tentacle portions whole.

3. Mix the dry ingredients on a plate or in a shallow bowl. In a separate bowl, beat the egg with a little water.

4. Dip the squid pieces into the egg mixture and then roll them in the flour mixture, shaking off any excess.

5. With a slotted spoon, carefully lower the squid into the hot oil. It will bubble quite a bit. Cook for 2 minutes, or until just golden and cooked through. Drain on paper towels and serve with lemon wedges and your favorite seafood sauce.

Marinated Grilled Squid Salad

One summer I was the cook on a sailing yacht in Portugal. I had been to the municipal fish market that morning, and I was looking for a way to cook squid very quickly to serve as a cold supper on what was a very hot day. The following preparation is a little like the technique for *escabesche*: cooking quickly, then marinating. It's lovely with a simple green salad and bread.

SERVES 4–6.

> 2 pounds cleaned squid, whole
> ½ cup olive oil
> ¼ cup crushed garlic
> 1 tablespoon chopped fresh oregano
> 1 tablespoon grated lemon rind
> 2 shallots, finely sliced
> ¼ cup white wine
> 3 tablespoons red wine vinegar
> Juice of 1 lemon
> Sea salt and freshly ground pepper, to taste

1. Combine the squid, oil, garlic, and oregano. Let the squid marinate for up to an hour.

2. Preheat a gas or charcoal grill to high. Place the squid on the grill until they're cooked through and a tiny bit charred. Flip over and cook briefly on the other side.

3. In a bowl, combine the remaining ingredients. Add the cooked squid to the bowl as they come off the grill. Refrigerate until ready to serve.

Swordfish

We are generally content not to know too much about where our food comes from. But two best-selling books, Sebastian Junger's *The Perfect Storm* and Linda Greenlaw's *The Hungry Ocean*, thrust swordfishing and commercial fishing in general into the American consciousness when they became bestsellers. *The Perfect Storm* gave a riveting account of the dangers of fishing: small boats in unpredictable and occasionally violent weather, far from shore. *The Hungry Ocean* speaks eloquently to the question of why, in the twenty-first century, people still choose what has often been called "the world's most dangerous occupation."

Of course, fishing has always been dangerous. Between 1870 and 1880, nearly 1,000 fishermen were lost at sea from Gloucester, Massachusetts, alone—a town with a population of only 15,000 souls.

For some people, fishing is in their blood and their heritage. Some need the structure and the discipline of shipboard life: For them, life ashore is always teetering on the edge of disaster. Safety lies at sea. For others, it's the elemental nature of fishing—the thrill of the chase—"killing fish" as Linda Greenlaw, considered by many to be the world's best swordfish boat captain, baldly put it. It's never the money. As Greenlaw's mentor explained to her, "If you're in it for the money, you're in the wrong business."

Greenlaw also has decided opinions on swordfish conservation. In *The Hungry Ocean,* she writes that "U.S. fishermen are not pirates. . . . Fishermen of my generation are conservation minded. We are also frustrated that the public is being brainwashed with misinformation by a group of do-gooders. Fishing for a living is our heritage. Consumers and seafood lovers should enjoy the fruits of the labor of law-abiding and conservation-minded fishermen without being made to feel guilty. Eat U.S.-caught swordfish! It's legal!"

Whatever your views about sustainability, it's generally agreed that fishing boats from other countries with less conservation-minded agendas have not helped the U.S. swordfishery much. This problem is exacerbated by the fact that swordfish are large and highly migratory. In the western Atlantic, swordfish range from Canada as far south as Argentina. In the eastern Atlantic, they range from Ireland to South Africa; they can also be found in the Indian and Pacific Oceans. The fact that these fish travel so widely and in so many international waters makes regulation that much more difficult. To further complicate matters, our demand for swordfish is so great that we end up importing a significant amount each year and can't be sure whether or not these fish have been caught in compliance with international regulations.

Government sources report that Atlantic swordfish stocks have rebounded and that the fishery is relatively stable. Good news for all of us who love our swordfish.

Swordfish are characterized by their long flat bill or sword. They have a prominent dorsal fin and reach a maximum size of 14 feet long; they can weigh more than 1,000 pounds. The meat is firm and perfect for grilling. It stands up well to seasonings and sauces but is wonderful just brushed with a little olive oil, seasoned with salt and pepper, and cooked briefly over hot coals.

> "In 1931, the Gloucester Times *published a photograph of the schooner* Mary D'Eon *with a swordfish impaled in its wooden bow. In 1967, the research submersible* Alvin *from Woods Hole Oceanographic Institution was hit by a swordfish off the east coast of Florida at a depth of 2,000 feet."*
>
> —Margaret Nagle, *UMaine Today*

The Florence

Mystic Seaport's dragger and summertime swordfishing boat *Florence* was built in 1926 just down the Mystic River below the drawbridge. At 40 feet, *Florence* is only half the size of Linda Greenlaw's *Hannah Boden*—but then the fishery was different eighty years ago. Swordfish swimming on the surface were harpooned from the long pulpit that extends from *Florence's* bow. A line was attached to the harpoon and to a wooden keg, which went overboard when a fish was struck. Usually a dory was then launched to retrieve the fish. *Florence* did not have to go far offshore to find swordfish. Now swordfishing boats range far out into the Atlantic to set their lines of baited hooks appropriately called long lines. The lines may run out as far as 40 miles, with massive hooks spread at intervals along the line.

The restored *Florence* is working to this day, carrying students to collect marine biology specimens from Fishers Island Sound.

Pan-Roasted Swordfish with Mustard-Herb Crust

SERVES 4.

2 teaspoons chopped Italian parsley

2 teaspoons chopped fresh oregano

2 teaspoons chopped fresh chives

2 teaspoons fresh thyme

2 teaspoons grated lemon zest

2 tablespoons horseradish mustard

2 tablespoons mayonnaise

1 tablespoon vegetable oil

1½ pounds swordfish steaks

1. In a bowl, whisk together the herbs, lemon zest, mustard, and mayonnaise.

2. Brush this mixture on the swordfish steaks and refrigerate for 20 minutes. Remove and let stand for 5 minutes.

3. In a grillpan or heavy skillet, heat the vegetable oil until it's hot but not smoking.

4. Add the swordfish steaks and cook until they're golden and crusty, about 4 to 5 minutes. Turn and cook for another 3 or 4 minutes, depending on the thickness of the steaks. The fish should be just opaque throughout.

Grilled Swordfish with Mint Gremolata

Gremolata is a traditional garnish/flavoring added to osso buco. It's a simple mixture of grated lemon rind, finely chopped or mashed garlic, and minced parsley. This wonderful combination is a natural for seafood, especially with the addition of aromatic mint leaves.

SERVES 4.

> 2 tablespoons finely chopped fresh flat-leaf parsley
> 1 tablespoon finely chopped fresh mint
> 2 teaspoons minced garlic (about 2 large cloves)
> 1½ teaspoons freshly grated lemon zest
> Freshly ground black pepper, to taste
> Sea salt, to taste
> 4 (6-ounce) swordfish steaks
> 2 tablespoons olive oil

1. Preheat a grill or broiler.

2. In a small bowl, stir together the gremolata ingredients and season with salt.

3. Brush the swordfish steaks with the olive oil, and season with salt and pepper to taste. Grill over high heat for 4 to 5 minutes.

4. Flip the fish over and top the cooked side of each steak with gremolata. Cook for an additional 4 to 5 minutes, until the fish is opaque throughout. Serve immediately.

Blackened Swordfish

This classic Cajun dish was made famous by New Orleans chef Paul Prud-homme. You can buy really good Cajun blackening spices (including Chef Paul's own brand) in the grocery store, but you can also make your own. Just increase the quantities given here to make extra, which you can store in an airtight container.

SERVES 4.

> 5 teaspoons paprika
> 1 teaspoon ground dried oregano
> 1 teaspoon ground dried thyme
> 1 teaspoon cayenne pepper (less or more to taste)
> 1 teaspoon garlic salt
> ½ teaspoon white pepper
> ½ teaspoon black pepper
> 4 (6-ounce) swordfish steaks
> 1 cup butter, melted

1. Combine all the dry ingredients well. Dump onto a plate or shallow bowl.

2. Preheat a skillet—preferably cast iron—until very hot. This may take 5 minutes or so. You want the pan to be almost red-hot.

3. Dip the steaks in the melted butter, and then coat both sides with the spice mixture. Place the steaks in the dry hot skillet (in batches, if necessary, so as not to crowd them), and cook for 2 minutes. Be careful—this will smoke a lot.

4. Flip the steaks over and cook the other side. Drizzle the remaining butter on the cooked side.

5. Flip the steaks again and cook for another 4 to 6 minutes, until they're just opaque throughout. Serve immediately, with any remaining butter poured over.

Tuna

Until fairly recently, it was understandable to think that tuna (aka "tunafish") came only in those hockey-puck-shaped cans with names like StarKist and Chicken of the Sea. Certainly when I was a kid, tuna meant a can of tuna. It meant a tunafish sandwich in my lunchbox. It never even occurred to me that tuna might come fresh—and certainly not that it might be eaten raw. Health issues notwithstanding, I am now a devotee of fresh tuna: raw, barely seared, grilled rare—you name it. I know, I know. There are numerous health debates about tuna raw or cooked, but it hasn't killed me yet. It hasn't even made me sick. (Nor has my love of steak tartare, but that's a topic for another book.)

Actually, canned tuna has an interesting history of its own. In 1903, A.P. Halfhill had a novel idea: He substituted canned tuna for canned sardines, the West Coast sardine stocks having suddenly disappeared. It was such a hit that it launched the San Diego offshore tuna-fishing fleet and later became a staple of soldiers in World War I. By the 1950s, the United States was the leading producer of canned tuna.

In New England, the tuna fishery relied not on canning but on fresh fish—both yellowfin and bluefin tuna. Sport fishing for tuna is an adventurous summertime activity—think *extreme fishing*. Commercially, many of the boats that fished for swordfish also

fished for tuna. The rigging was the same as was the technique—harpooning from a long pulpit off the bow of the boat. Mystic Seaport's fishing boat *Star*, built in 1950 in nearby Noank, is just such a vessel. For nearly thirty years, she fished for both swordfish and tuna out of Montauk, New York.

In other parts of the world, tuna has been a favorite for thousands of years. Professor Daniel Levine noted in his speech "Tuna in the Ancient World" to the American Institute of Wine and Food that "One of the earliest references to [tuna's] attractive flavor comes from the sixth-century BCE poet Hipponax, who wrote about a man who literally wasted his life by luxuriously overindulging in tuna with a savory sauce:

"'For one of them, dining at his ease and lavishly every day on tuna and savory sauce [*myssotos*] like a eunuch from Lampsacus, ate up his inheritance; as a result he has to dig a rocky hillside, munching on cheap figs and coarse barley bread, fodder for slaves.'"

Tunny fish, as it was known in the 1800s, was prized as a rare catch, especially by immigrants from the Mediterranean. The relatively few people who had access to fresh tuna seemed to value it, but it wasn't until canning became an option and the Pacific tuna fishery and canneries began to thrive in the 1920s that it became a common addition to the American diet. Just imagine the 1950s and '60s without tuna casseroles!

While tuna does make an excellent sandwich or casserole (tuna casserole is kind of a retro guilty pleasure of mine), tuna is once again haute cuisine. Sushi, sashimi, grilled, baked, marinated—tuna is the delicacy that the ancient Greeks appreciated.

Tuna Tartare in Endive Boats

MAKES 18 HORS D'OEUVRES.

- ½ pound sushi-grade tuna
- ¾ teaspoon grated fresh ginger
- 3 tablespoons tamari or soy sauce
- 1 teaspoon wasabi paste (or more to taste)
- 1 tablespoon rice wine vinegar or sushi vinegar
- 4 scallions, chopped
- 18 Belgian endive leaves, separated and washed

1. Chop the tuna into small pieces—about a ¼-inch dice. Gently mix in the remaining ingredients.

2. Place a spoonful of the tartare on each endive leaf. Serve chilled.

Sam Hayward's Tuna and Green Bean Salad

Sam Hayward's award-winning Portland, Maine, restaurant, Fore Street, has become an icon in what *Bon Appétit* called America's Foodiest Small Town. This is his unique take on a classic *salade niçoise*. The tuna is "marinated" overnight and then baked in extra-virgin olive oil and served with lightly cooked green beans and fresh summer lettuce. Plan on making the tuna a day or two ahead of time.

SERVES 4–6.

Tuna

1 pound very fresh tuna, preferably yellowfin

1½ tablespoons Maine sea salt

Freshly ground black pepper, to taste

2 cloves garlic, very thinly sliced

A few fresh thyme sprigs

About 1–2 cups extra-virgin olive oil

Beans and Vinaigrette

8 ounces green beans, ends trimmed

3 tablespoons sherry vinegar

¾ cup extra-virgin olive oil

Salt and fresh black pepper, to taste

2 tablespoons chopped summer garden herbs, such as flat parsley, thyme, rosemary, marjoram or oregano, mint, etc.

3 cups fresh summer lettuce, such as Bibb, Reine des Glaces, Lolla Rossa, or salad bowl.

1. To prepare the tuna, place it in a bowl or plastic container and rub with the salt and pepper. Toss the garlic and thyme sprigs on top, cover tightly, and refrigerate for 24 to 48 hours, turning the fish at least once.

2. Preheat the oven to 300°F. Place the tuna in a baking dish or shallow roasting pan and cover with the olive oil. Bake for 15 minutes. Reduce the oven temperature to 275°F and bake for about 45 minutes. The tuna is done when it flakes easily when tested with a fork. Cool the tuna in the fat; refrigerate after it comes to room temperature.

3. To prepare the beans, fill a pot with lightly salted water and bring it to a boil over high heat. Cook the beans for 2 minutes; drain and place in a bowl of ice-cold water. Drain again.

4. To prepare the vinaigrette, whisk together the vinegar, oil, salt, pepper, and herbs in a bowl.

5. Remove the tuna from the oil and break it into large pieces.

6. Toss the beans with the lettuce, adding enough of the vinaigrette to lightly coat the leaves. Arrange on a serving plate. Add the tuna on top and drizzle with a little of the vinaigrette. Serve any additional vinaigrette on the side.

Seared Tuna in a Black and White Sesame Crust

SERVES 4.

6 tablespoons soy sauce, divided

2 tablespoons toasted sesame oil

1 teaspoon ginger paste (available in the Asian food sections of many markets)

1 pound sushi-grade tuna steak, 1–1½ inches thick

3 tablespoons black sesame seeds

3 tablespoons white sesame seeds

1 teaspoon peanut oil

Wasabi, to taste

1. In a bowl, whisk together 2 tablespoons of the soy sauce, along with the sesame oil and ginger paste.

2. Cut the tuna into rectangular "logs" 1 to 1½ inches wide, 1½ inches high, and about 4 inches long. Thoroughly coat the tuna in the soy mixture. Cover and refrigerate for up to an hour.

3. In a wide bowl or on a plate, combine the black and white sesame seeds.

4. Rub a cast-iron or other heavy skillet with the peanut oil and heat until very hot.

5. Using tongs, add the tuna to pan and cook for just 2 minutes on each side, until the outside is crisp and the inside is rare. Serve with the remaining soy sauce and wasabi as you would for sushi.

BOUNTY
OF THE LAND

Fruit

Apples

"Even if I knew that tomorrow the world would go to pieces, I would still plant my apple tree."

Martin Luther

I can hardly imagine what it must have been like to step ashore on New England soil (or snow) after a long and probably uncomfortable journey across the Atlantic. The bounty of the land must have been hard to spot, especially if you arrived in winter. But the first European settlers were a hardy lot—I would have been on the next ship home. And fortunately, the indigenous people saw fit to teach the settlers how to survive, a debt that was never and can never be repaid. Europeans lucky enough to arrive in the fall would have been delighted by the glorious apple trees bearing sweet, nutritional fruit.

Apples seem to symbolize a beginning from seed and maturity in a plentiful harvest. Whether part of a savory or sweet dish, juiced, fermented, sauced, dried, or jellied, apples are one of the most versatile foods we eat.

At most supermarkets, commercial, mass-produced apples come in a number of familiar varieties: Red Delicious, Golden Delicious, Macintosh, Cortland, Granny Smith to name a few. As most cooks know, each variety has its own superpowers, whether for cooking, juicing, or eating cold and crisp, "out of hand."

Heirloom apples, thanks to the efforts of a number of dedicated growers, are being preserved for the future so we can still find the descendants of some of the earliest apples cultivated in this country. Although most of us would recognize the commercially produced varieties named above, which are produced in the millions of bushels, these varieties lack the poetic character of names like Hidden Rose, Pink Pearl, Sierra Beauty, Opalescent, or Ambrosia. We owe a debt of gratitude to these curators of our apple history.

Settlers brought seeds, or pippins, of their favorites. They were then crossed with native crabapples with guidance from the Native people, sometimes by cross-pollination and sometimes by grafting, which produced a sweeter, larger, more versatile fruit. Over the years, many varieties evolved due to careful husbandry, New England's terroir, and a good deal of help from Mother Nature. The Roxbury Russet is considered to be the oldest cultivated apple variety, dating back to the 1640s.

Apple Dumplings

Clarkdale Farm, a fourth generation orchard in Deerfield, Massachusetts, produces more than 40 varieties of heirloom apples. This recipe is one of their signature dishes—a kind of apple jelly roll with a brown sugar topping like a cinnamon bun.

SERVES 6-8.

Dumplings

3 cups flour

1 cup shortening

½ cup cold water

½ teaspoon salt

5 tart crisp (preferably heirloom) apples, peeled and sliced

⅔ cup sugar

1 teaspoon ground cinnamon

½ teaspoon nutmeg

Topping

3 cups brown sugar, lightly packed

3 cups boiling water

2 tablespoons butter

1. Preheat oven to 350°F. In a mixing bowl, combine the first four ingredients and mix together until a dough forms.

2. Roll thin like a piecrust into a rectangular shape. Toss the sliced apples with the sugar, cinnamon, and nutmeg.

3. Mix well and spread on the dough. Roll the dough up like a jelly roll and slice into 12 pieces. Place in a 9 x 13-inch baking pan.

4. To make the topping, in a separate bowl, mix the brown sugar, boiling water, and butter and stir until blended. Pour over the apple rolls. Bake for 30 to 40 minutes. Serve with cream or ice cream.

Scott Farm's Tarte Tatin

Scott Farm Orchard in Dummerston, Vermont, is a sort of shrine to heirloom apples. Zeke Goodband, the "orchardist," has a passion for heirloom apples in their many incarnations.

SERVES 6-8.

> ½ **stick of butter**
>
> 1 **cup vanilla sugar (Place a vanilla bean in a jar with a cup of sugar and leave for a few days.)**
>
> 8 **Calville Blanc d'Hiver apples, or other firm, tart apples**
>
> 1 **unbaked pie crust**

1. In a 14-inch frying pan, melt the butter over medium heat. Add the vanilla sugar and stir until golden brown. Remove from the heat and set aside.

2. Peel, quarter, and core the apples. Cut the quarters in half lengthwise and place them, overlapping, on top of the caramelized sugar.

3. Cover loosely with pie crust. Do not press crust to edge of pan.

4. Preheat oven to 400ºF and bake for 45 minutes. Cool in the pan.

5. Cover the frying pan with a dish or platter. Holding the pan and platter firmly between both hands, turn upside down. Serve warm.

Arugula Salad with Sliced Apples, Shaved Beets, Toasted Walnuts, and Goat Cheese

This recipe, and the one following, first appeared in *Northeast Flavor* magazine. It was developed by Contributing Editor Paula Sullivan, chef, food writer, recipe developer, and tester.

SERVES 2–4.

> 6 cups baby arugula
>
> 2 apples, peeled, cored, halved, and sliced thin (about 3 cups)
>
> 1 medium beet, peeled and shaved into thin chips with a vegetable peeler or mandolin (about 1½ cups)
>
> 3 tablespoons apple cider vinaigrette (recipe follows)
>
> Salt and black pepper, to taste
>
> 4 ounces soft goat cheese

1. Place all ingredients except goat cheese in a large bowl and toss gently to combine.

2. Crumble goat cheese over the top. Serve immediately.

Apple Cider

More than the sum of its parts, apple cider has its own importance: as a cool, crisp fall drink; as vinegar; as fermented cider; and as cider molasses, an important sweetener when blackstrap molasses was not on hand.

Apple Cider Vinaigrette

MAKES ABOUT 1¼ CUPS.

> 1 cup apple cider
> ¼ teaspoon dried thyme
> ¼ cup apple cider vinegar
> 1 tablespoon Dijon mustard
> 1 tablespoon honey
> 1 small shallot, minced
> ½ cup vegetable oil
> Salt and black pepper, to taste

1. In a small saucepan, bring the cider to a boil with the thyme. Reduce the heat and let simmer until the volume is reduced to ¼ cup. Let cool for 10 minutes and transfer to a blender.

2. Add the remaining ingredients and process until smooth. Chill and shake well before serving.

Baked Onion Apple Cider Soup with Smoked Cheddar Cheese Gratiné

This heartwarming fall soup comes from Chef Jeff Paige, who virtually founded the farm-to-table movement in New Hampshire. His restaurant, Cotton, in Manchester, New Hampshire, is a favorite of mine.

SERVES 6-8.

> 1 stick unsalted butter
>
> 5 medium onions, peeled and thinly sliced
>
> 4 cups beef stock
>
> 4 cups fresh apple cider
>
> 2 teaspoons minced fresh thyme
>
> ¼ cup light brown sugar (omit if cider is sweet enough)
>
> Kosher salt and freshly ground black pepper, to taste
>
> Butter as needed for spreading
>
> 6–8 slices French bread, ¼-inch thick
>
> 6–8 slices gruyère or swiss cheese
>
> 2 cups grated smoked Vermont cheddar or traditional cheddar cheese

1. In a large saucepan, melt the butter over medium-low heat. Add the onions and cook until well caramelized, about 20 to 30 minutes, taking care not to burn them.

2. Add the stock, cider, and thyme, and bring to a boil, then lower the heat and simmer the soup for 1½ hours. Skim any foam off the top periodically.

3. Season with the brown sugar, if needed, and salt and pepper. The soup may be made up to this point a day ahead and kept covered in the refrigerator.

4. To make the croutons, lightly butter the slices of French bread and broil until toasted on both sides.

5. To serve, preheat the oven to 400°F. Place six to eight ovenproof soup cups or crocks in a large roasting pan and fill them with the hot soup. Pour hot water into the roasting pan to come halfway up the sides of the cups or crocks.

6. Top each cup or crock of soup with a crouton, a slice of gruyère cheese, and ⅓ to ¼ cup of grated cheddar.

7. Bake the soup until the cheese is golden brown and the soup is hot and bubbly. Serve immediately.

Apple Cider Molasses

This is also known as Boiled Cider. Making it is a very simple process but does require your attention. It is a matter of reducing apple cider by one-third to one-fifth of its original volume. It takes a while depending on your pot and heat level. Keep a close eye on the cider after it has reduced by half. From there on, the reduction process can move quite quickly, turning the cider into a hard, amber-colored mess.

MAKES 4 CUPS.

> **1 gallon fresh apple cider**

In a deep, heavy pot, boil the apple cider over medium-high heat. Mark a wooden spoon or chopstick at the level of the fresh cider in the pot. Mark this section into quarters. Boil until the cider is reduced by three-quarters.

Blueberries

"I may never be happy but tonight I am content. Nothing more than an empty house, the warm hazy weariness from a day spent setting strawberry runners in the sun, a glass of cool, sweet milk and a shallow dish of blueberries bathed in cream."

—Sylvia Plath

Blueberries are one of America's original wild fruits. In New England, they are virtually a culinary icon with a history of creative uses—and some pretty funny names. There is Blueberry Slump, Blueberry Buckle, and Blueberry Grunt. All are variations on a theme.

Although blueberries have been picked wild forever, it was only when a native of New Jersey, a Quaker by the name of Elizabeth White, worked with agricultural scientist Frederick Coville that a crop was created. Most people believed that blueberries couldn't be cultivated, but what White and Coville discovered was the blueberries did not grow well in typically rich farm soils. They preferred acidic, scrubby, sandy conditions. Through trial and error and multiple graftings, their work was successful, and in 1910 blueberries became an important crop. Fittingly, it is the state fruit of New Jersey, but Maine could well have claimed it.

Blueberry Grunt

This is practically the national dish of some of our neighbors to the north like Nova Scotia and Cape Breton, but it was popular in New England as well. It's a great old-timey dish with a very homey (if perplexing) name.

SERVES 6.

4 cups blueberries (frozen or fresh)

1 cup sugar

1 cup water

¼ teaspoon cinnamon

¼ teaspoon nutmeg

1 teaspoon fresh lemon juice

2 cups flour

1 cup sugar

2 teaspoons baking powder

1 teaspoon salt

2 tablespoons butter

1 cup buttermilk

1. In a medium pan, combine the berries, sugar, and water. Bring to a boil and then reduce to a simmer until the liquid has thickened. Remove from the heat, add the cinnamon, nutmeg, and lemon juice, and set aside.

2. Combine the flour, sugar, baking powder, and salt in a bowl. Cut in the butter, then add the milk and combine until just mixed—do not overmix.

3. Roll the flour mixture into balls and drop them into the berry mixture. Place the pan on medium heat, cover, and simmer for 15 minutes. Do not lift the lid—the biscuit topping is steaming itself in the berry juices.

4. Top with fresh mint leaves. Serve warm with whipped cream or ice cream.

Ellie's Famous Blueberry Cake

There are more than 44,000 acres of wild blueberries growing in Maine, and while not strictly cultivated as a crop, the wild blueberries have been harvested by companies like Wyman's of Maine, who have also perfected freezing berries. The farm in Maine covers more than 10,000 acres of rocky, scrubby ground, which their blueberries seem to enjoy very much. This is their recipe for Blueberry Cake.

SERVES 8-10.

Cake
¾ cup sugar

½ cup butter

1 egg, beaten

½ cup milk

2 cups flour

½ teaspoon salt

2 teaspoons baking powder

2 cups blueberries (preferably Wyman's Frozen Wild Blueberries)

Topping
½ cup sugar

⅓ cup flour

1 teaspoon cinnamon

¼ cup butter, softened

1. Preheat the oven to 375°F.

2. Cream together the sugar and butter. Mix in the egg and milk.

3. Sift together the dry ingredients and add to the butter mixture, alternating with the liquid. Fold in the blueberries.

4. Pour the batter into a greased 9 x 9-inch pan.

5. For the topping, sift together the sugar, flour, and cinnamon.

6. Cut in the butter until it forms lumps the size of peas.

7. Spread the topping over the cake batter, and bake for 30 to 40 minutes.

Blueberry Balsamic Glaze

This is a great accompaniment to your favorite meat dishes, especially pork and poultry.

MAKES 1 CUP.

½ **cup frozen or fresh blueberries**

2 **tablespoons water**

1 **tablespoon red vermouth**

1 **tablespoon honey**

½ **cup balsamic vinegar**

1. Place the blueberries and water in a medium saucepan on medium heat. Using a wooden spoon or potato masher, begin breaking the blueberries while cooking.

2. Add the vermouth and honey. The blueberries will begin to boil and the sauce will begin to thicken. Stir in the balsamic vinegar. Bring the sauce to a boil and reduce to a syrupy consistency. (Watch carefully; the reduction can turn to a cement-like substance in a matter of minutes and get the smoke detector shrieking. Trust me on this.)

Cherries

There is a noticeable lack of cherry recipes in vintage cookbooks. Part of the reason may be that black cherries contain cyanide in parts other than actual flesh. These cherries were, however, used to flavor liquor.

Rum Cherries

These would be good over ice cream, or as a base for mulled wine.

MAKES 2½ CUPS.

> **2 cups pitted and halved cherries**
>
> **3 tablespoons white sugar**
>
> **1⅛ cups water**
>
> **¼ cup rum**

1. Combine cherries, sugar, and water in a medium saucepan. Heat until sugar is melted.

2. Allow mixture to cool a bit. Add rum and refrigerate until ready to use.

Cherry and Plum Slump

This recipe comes from award-winning chef Daniel Bruce, executive chef at the Boston Harbor Hotel and founder of the annual Boston Wine Festival. He has been recognized twice as one of the Best Hotel Chefs in America by the James Beard Foundation. His cookbook, *Chef Daniel Bruce Simply New England: Seasonal Recipes That Celebrate Land and Sea* (Lyons Press, 2013), included some of his most wonderful recipes: creative and cutting edge but always seeming to pay homage to classic New England ingredients and recipes.

SERVES 6.

> ### Biscuits
> **1 cup all-purpose flour**
>
> **1 teaspoon baking powder**
>
> **3 tablespoons sugar**
>
> **½ teaspoon nutmeg**
>
> **½ teaspoon ground fennel**
>
> **Pinch of salt**
>
> **3 tablespoons cold butter, cut into small pieces**
>
> **⅓ cup milk**

Fruit

4 plums, pitted and cut into quarters

1 cup cherries, pitted

½ cup sugar

1 teaspoon vanilla extract

¼ cup water

2 tablespoons chopped fresh mint

1. Sift the flour, baking powder, sugar, nutmeg, ground fennel, and salt into a medium-sized bowl.

2. Add the butter, and mix with your hands only until the butter crumbles to the size of peas.

3. Stir in the milk, and mix until a batter begins to form. Don't overmix.

4. To make the slump, in a medium-sized saucepan over medium-high heat, bring the plums, cherries, sugar, vanilla extract, and water to a boil. Lower the heat and simmer for 4 minutes. Stir in the mint.

5. Drop 6 tablespoons of the biscuit dough over the simmering fruit, allowing a small space between each spoonful of dough.

6. Cover and slowly simmer for 10 minutes. Serve immediately.

Cranberries

"The Indians and English use them much, boyling them with Sugar for Sauce to eat with their Meat, and it is a delicious sauce."
—John Josselyn, while visiting New England in 1663

Cranberries are one of the handful of fruits native to New England. As it happens, on this fall day, I am lucky enough to have just come from picking wild cranberries. (Seriously.) Our friend Dudley took us bushwhacking through wild roses, scrub, and marsh grass to a wild bog, whose location is a closely guarded secret. We picked more than 2 gallons. It is, however, hard work. I can see why people were eager to cultivate them.

According to the Cape Cod Cranberry Growers Association, "Wampanoag People across southeastern Massachusetts have enjoyed the annual harvest of *sasumuneash*—wild cranberries—for 12,000 years. Some ate berries fresh while others dried them to make *nasampe* (grits) or pemmican—a mix of berries, dried meat and animal fat which could last for months."

We first cultivated cranberries in Dennis, Massachusetts, in 1816. Today, the biggest grower, Ocean Spray, is actually a cooperative of 700 growers.

Wild Rice–Cranberry Soup

This recipe comes from *A Beautiful Bowl of Soup* by Paulette Mitchell (Chronicle Books, 2004).

Wild rice is actually an aquatic grain-like seed rather than a rice. It grows in marshy bogs, lakes, and rivers and is also an indigenous plant. In this soup, it is paired with tart-sweet cranberries and sherry to add elegance. (If only I could find a wild rice paddy next to the cranberry bog!)

SERVES 4–6 (ABOUT 5 CUPS).

4 tablespoons unsalted butter

1 carrot, finely chopped

1 celery stalk, finely chopped

½ cup finely chopped onion

3 tablespoons all-purpose flour

3 cups vegetable stock

1½ cups cooked wild rice

½ cup dried cranberries

1 cup milk or half-and-half

2 tablespoons dry sherry (optional)

Salt and freshly ground pepper, to taste

¼ cup fresh parsley, chopped

1. Melt the butter in a Dutch oven over medium heat. Add the carrot, celery, and onion; cook, stirring occasionally, until the carrot is tender, about 8 minutes.

2. Add the flour and stir until smooth. Gradually add the vegetable stock, whisking constantly to prevent lumps. Increase the heat to medium-high, and stir until the soup is thickened, about 5 minutes. Stir in the rice and cranberries. Reduce the heat, cover, and simmer, stirring occasionally, until the cranberries are softened and plumped, about 15 minutes.

3. Stir in the milk and sherry. Stir occasionally until warmed through.

4. Season with salt and pepper to taste.

5. Sprinkle each serving with parsley and serve.

Note: This soup will keep for up to 3 days in a covered container in the refrigerator. When reheating, stir in milk to thin as desired.

Tip: To cook wild rice, first rinse it in a strainer under cold running water or in a bowl of water; drain. Bring 2 cups water, ½ cup rice, and ½ teaspoon salt to a boil in a heavy saucepan over medium-high heat. Reduce the heat, cover, and simmer until the rice kernels are opened and slightly chewy rather than mushy, 45 to 55 minutes; drain well. Makes about 1½ cups.

Uncle's Spiced Cranberry Jelly

When our nieces were little girls, they seemed to like my husband's cranberry jelly better than just about anything else on the Thanksgiving table. We always made extra so they could take some home. This is an amped-up version of the recipe that appears in *The Fannie Farmer Cookbook*.

MAKES ABOUT 4 CUPS.

> 3 cups water
> 24 ounces cranberries
> 1 orange, quartered
> 1 piece stick cinnamon
> 3 whole cloves
> 4 cups sugar

1. In a medium saucepan, boil the water, cranberries, orange, cinnamon stick, and cloves until the berries begin to soften and pop, about 15 minutes.

2. Push the cranberry mixture through a sieve. Return the mixture to the pot, add the sugar, and simmer until smooth and thickened, 3 to 5 minutes. Pour the jelly into nonreactive bowls, and chill until gelled.

Cranberry, Banana, and White Chocolate Muffins

Until recently, I rarely attempted baking. The cake I tried to make for my father's 70th birthday could definitely have been called a "slump." But I had the good fortune to be invited to a food writers' weekend at King Arthur Flour's Baking Education Center, and the instructors were so great that I believed I might be able to bake something simple. This recipe is one I've adapted from their cookbook, *The King Arthur Flour Baker's Companion*.

MAKES 12 MUFFINS.

8 tablespoons unsalted butter

1 cup granulated sugar

1 large egg

½ teaspoon nutmeg

½ teaspoon allspice

2 medium ripe bananas, mashed

⅓ cup milk

1 cup white whole-wheat flour

1 cup unbleached all-purpose flour

1½ teaspoons baking powder

½ teaspoon baking soda

½ teaspoon salt

½ cup white chocolate chips

½ cup chopped walnuts.

1 cup dried, sweetened cranberries

1. Preheat the oven to 350°F.

2. In a medium bowl, cream together the butter and sugar until smooth. Scrape the bowl down and beat in the egg, spices, bananas, and milk.

3. In a separate bowl, whisk together the dry ingredients, then gently stir them into the butter mixture.

4. Stir in the chocolate chips, walnuts, and cranberries.

5. Pour the batter evenly among 12 muffin cups, and bake for 25 minutes, or until a toothpick stuck into the center of a muffin comes out clean. Allow to cool a bit, and place them on a plate and serve.

Peaches

"Here are also Peaches, and very good, and in great quantities, not an Indian Plantation without them..."

—William Penn

There is something of a controversy about whether peaches are native to North America, but reports like those above reference "Indian orchards" and "Indian plantations." Others argue that the first peach trees were grown by early settlers. I'm only a hobby historian, but if I had to venture a guess, I would say that, like apples, there was a native species that may well have been grafted with English strains to produce a fruit much like what we have today.

In late summer and early fall, if you are lucky enough to find mature peach trees like those on K Farm in Kingston, New Hampshire, the harvest is abundant if short-lived, and the scent of warm sun on windfall peaches is heady indeed. Picking peaches on a fine fall day is pretty close to heaven.

Peach Butter

Apple butter may be more familiar and more readily available, but during the brief season when peaches in New England are perfectly ripe, you just have to find a way to bottle that late summer harvest.

MAKES 3 PINTS.

> 8 pounds fresh, ripe peaches
>
> 2⅔ cup granulated sugar
>
> ½ cup fresh orange juice
>
> 4 cinnamon sticks
>
> ½ teaspoon kosher or sea salt

1. Using a sharp knife, score each peach with a shallow X shape on the bottom. Fill a large pot (at least 5 quarts) with water and bring to a boil over high heat. Add the peaches and boil until the skins loosen, about 1 minute.

2. Remove the peaches from the water with a slotted spoon, and run cold water over them to stop the cooking. The peaches should now slip easily out of their skins. Discard the skins.

3. Using a knife or your hands, break the peaches into large pieces and put them in a 6-quart slow cooker. Add the sugar, orange juice, cinnamon sticks, and salt, and stir.

4. Set the heat to high and cover the slow cooker; cook until the mixture is simmering, 1 to 1½ hours. Reduce the heat to low and leave the lid slightly ajar. Cook until the peach butter is thick and mahogany-colored, 7 to 9 hours. If you want to preserve the butter, pour it into sterilized jars and process for 10 minutes in a boiling-water bath.

Peach and Blueberry Crisp

On a whim, I swapped peaches and blueberries for apples, as both looked great at our local farmers' market. But you could use this basic crisp recipe with almost any fruit.

SERVES 6.

½ cup butter (1 stick), plus enough to butter baking dish

3 cups peaches, peeled and sliced

3 cups blueberries

⅓ cup water

¾ cup flour

1 cup brown sugar

½ teaspoon cinnamon

¼ cup rolled oats

⅛ cup wheat germ

1. Preheat the oven to 350°F. Butter a deep 9" x 9" baking dish.

2. Arrange the prepared fruit in the bottom of the baking dish and add water.

3. Mix the flour, sugar, cinnamon, oats, wheat germ, and butter. Spread over the fruit, and bake for 20 to 25 minutes, until topping is crisp and brown. Serve with ice cream or whipped cream.

Grilled Peaches with Molten Chocolate

This is hardly a classic or traditional recipe, but it is one of my favorite things to serve to guests.

SERVES 6.

6 firm but ripe peaches

2 tablespoons brown sugar or molasses

4 tablespoons butter, melted

1 large bittersweet or dark chocolate bar (about 3 ounces), broken into 12 pieces

1. Cut the peaches in half and remove the pits. Mix the sugar or molasses into the melted butter.

2. Place the peaches skin-side down on a baking sheet, and brush with sweetened butter.

3. Place them under a low broiler or put them flesh-side down on a grill. If using a grill, flip the peaches when just caramelized.

4. Place a piece of chocolate in the middle of each peach and cook until the chocolate melts. Top each with a dollop of ice cream.

Strawberries

"Strawberries that in garden grow
Are plump and juicy fine,
But sweeter far as wise men know
Spring from the woodland vine."

—Robert Graves

One of the first things to impress settlers arriving on our shores was the abundance of strawberries in early summer. In fact, in Portsmouth, New Hampshire, near where I live, is the wonderful re-creation of a historic village called Strawbery Banke (*sic*), named for the bright red berries that once grew by the banks of the Piscataqua River. Even today, near my house, if I time it right, I can find wild strawberries growing.

Easy Strawberry Shortcake

This recipe comes from food photographer, blogger, and recipe developer Ali Goodwin.

SERVES 6.

Strawberry Topping

1 quart (4 cups) strawberries, sliced

¼ cup sugar

Shortcakes

2⅓ cups Original Bisquick mix

½ cup milk

¼ cup sugar

3 tablespoons butter, melted

½ cup whipping cream

1. Heat the oven to 425°F. In a large bowl, mash the strawberries and ¼ cup sugar; set aside.

2. For the shortcake, in a medium bowl, stir the Bisquick mix, milk, ¼ cup sugar, and the butter until a soft dough forms. On an ungreased cookie sheet, drop dough by (6) spoonfuls.

3. Bake 10 to 12 minutes, or until golden brown. Meanwhile, in a small bowl, beat the whipping cream with an electric mixer on high speed until soft peaks form.

4. Serve the shortcakes warm topped with strawberries and whipped cream.

Strawberry Ice Cream

Though it's not likely this was the texture that we're used to today, in 1841, Sara Josepha Hale recorded this recipe in *The Good Housekeeper*. Isinglass was used as thickener. Today we would substitute plain gelatin.

"Mix one pound of Strawberry juice, strained and sweetened, with one pint of whipped cream; if it is to be frozen in a mould, add a little isinglass, melted and strained. If to be eaten in glasses, isinglass is not necessary."

Vegetables and Legumes

"*The first gatherings of the garden in May of salads, radishes, and herbs made me feel like a mother about her baby—how could anything so beautiful be mine. And this emotion of wonder filled me for each vegetable as it was gathered every year. There is nothing that is comparable to it, as satisfactory or as thrilling, as gathering the vegetables one has grown.*"

—Alice B. Toklas

Glazed Root Vegetables

Single vegetables as well as combinations can be glazed and roasted this way, including celery root, onions, beets, parsnips, and turnips. Though brussels sprouts are not root vegetables, they are a hardy crop and can be picked well into the cold weather.

SERVES 6–8.

> 4 carrots, scraped and cut into 1-inch dice
>
> 1 rutabaga, peeled and cut into 1-inch dice
>
> ¾ pound brussels sprouts, outer leaves removed and cut in half
>
> ¾ pound small boiling onions
>
> 1 teaspoon salt, plus ½ teaspoon kosher or sea salt, divided
>
> ½ stick butter
>
> 2 tablespoons sugar
>
> ¼ teaspoon black pepper
>
> ¼ teaspoon nutmeg
>
> ¼ teaspoon mace
>
> ¼ cup olive oil

1. Preheat the oven to 425°F. Place the roasting pan in the oven to preheat. Preheating the pan prior to adding the vegetables will prevent them from sticking to the pan.

2. Prepare the carrots and rutabaga. Rinse the brussels sprouts and onions.

3. In a large pot, bring 2 quarts of water to a boil and add 1 teaspoon salt. Blanch each group of vegetables separately, boiling 3 to 5 minutes, and place each in cold water to stop the cooking process. Remove the skins from the onions.

4. Heat the butter and oil in a skillet with the sugar, remaining salt, pepper, nutmeg, and mace.

5. In a medium bowl, toss the blanched vegetables to coat them in the butter, oil, and seasonings.

6. Place the vegetables in the preheated roasting pan and bake for 45 minutes, or until browned and fork tender.

Beans

Award-winning author and food historian Sandra Oliver writes, "Martha Ballard, a mid-wife, homemaker, and prodigious gardener in Augusta, Maine, wrote in her diary that she planted, '8 kinds of Beens in ye South end of ye corn field.' Elsewhere in her twenty-year daily record, Ballard reported on growing, gathering, shelling, sorting, and Cooking Sun, Crambury, Hundred to One, Scarlet, Poland, Wild Goose, and brown beans. Even in Ballard's time, these were heirlooms—that is, beans handed down in families from the earliest settlements, acquired from the Native Americans for whom, along with corn and squash, the beans were a staple crop."

Nutritionally, beans are a superfood: low in fat, full of fiber, and high in vitamins and minerals.

> "The countrie aboundeth naturally with store of roots of great varietie and good to eat. Our turnips, parsnips, and carrots are here both bigger and sweeter than is ordinary to be found in England. Here are stores of pompions, cowcumbers, and other things of that nature which I know not..."
>
> —Reverend Francis Higginson, in his book
> *New-England's Plantation*

Baked Beans

You'd be hard pressed to come up with a dish more closely associated with New England than baked beans. America's two oldest Boston (aka Beantown) restaurants, the Union Oyster House and Durgin Park, are both famous for theirs. And bean suppers are a long-standing tradition in many towns and villages. Bean hole cooking is perhaps the oldest method of cooking and is a bit labor intensive for most. But at various fairs, including the Maine Organic Farmers and Growers Association (MOFGA), you can witness the beans cooked in a pit (or hole) over hot coals and then buried. They may cook for as much as 22 hours. It's a lot of work, but like other New England traditions such as clambakes, you're not just eating great food, you're reenacting history.

SERVES 8-10.

1 pound dried Yellow Eye, Northern, or White Pea beans

2 quarts of water

¼ pound lean salt pork

1 small onion, diced

½ cup molasses, or more to taste

1 cup tomato juice

1 tablespoon dry mustard

1 tablespoon brown sugar

1 teaspoon garlic or onion powder

1 teaspoon salt

1 teaspoon ground pepper

1. Soak the beans in the water overnight, then drain.

2. In the morning, preheat the oven to 300°F. Bring the beans to a boil and cook for 15 to 20 minutes, or until the skins start to burst. Drain and reserve the liquid.

3. Slash the pork (but not through the rind) in ½-inch cubic sections. Put the pork in an ovenproof pot with the onions and cooked beans.

4. Add the molasses, tomato juice, mustard, brown sugar, garlic or onion powder, salt, and pepper, and enough of the reserved cooking water to the pot so that you see it barely below the surface of the beans at the top.

5. Bake for 5 to 6 hours at 300°F. Check occasionally to see that the liquid remains; add a little boiling water as needed without drowning the beans. For the last hour, use a fork to pull the pork to the surface of the pot, and bake with the lid off to allow the pork to brown.

Jacob's Cattle Bean Stew
with Fennel and Swiss Chard

Todd Heberlein, executive chef at Volante Farms in Needham, Massachusetts, provided us with these great heirloom bean recipes. Known as "a place for all seasons," Volante Farms has been family owned and operated since 1917. The farm also has a deli, bakery, farm kitchen, catering facility, and extensive greenhouses. They also host special community events like chili cook-offs and craft beer dinners.

SERVES 4.

1 pound Jacob's Cattle beans, soaked overnight

2 bay leaves

Salt and pepper, to taste

1 yellow onion, thinly sliced

1 fennel bulb, thinly sliced

1 cup pitted green olives

1 whole Meyer lemon, seeds removed, diced

2 tablespoons chopped garlic

1 tablespoon herbes de Provence

Extra-virgin olive oil, as needed

1 red bell pepper, diced

1 bunch swiss chard, chopped

2 teaspoons fresh lemon juice

1 tablespoon chopped parsley

1. Preheat the oven to 350°F.

2. Place the beans in a large pot with the bay leaves and enough water to cover by a few inches. Bring to a boil, then reduce to a simmer. Cook until just tender, about an hour. Season with salt and pepper. Drain the beans, reserving 1 cup of broth. Set aside.

3. In a bowl, mix together onions, fennel, olives, lemon, garlic, herbes de Provence, a pinch of salt and pepper, and enough oil to lightly coat the mixture. Spread out on a sheet pan and roast in the oven until golden brown and tender, about 15 to 20 minutes. Set aside.

4. Add a few tablespoons of oil to a wide-bottomed pot. Add the bell pepper and sauté for 1 minute. Add the swiss chard and reserved bean broth and cook until just wilted, about 2 minutes. Add in the beans, vegetable mixture, lemon juice, and parsley. Drizzle olive oil over the top, and season to taste.

Corn

"I have no hostility to nature, but a child's love to it. I expand and live in the warm day like corn and melons."

—Ralph Waldo Emerson

The corn that was growing in New England when the settlers arrived was not the sweet corn that we treasure in summer and fall. The hard corn grown was used primarily for meal that was then used for porridges, breads, and other foods. These recipes make use of sweet corn, which was cultivated sometime in the 1700s.

Succotash

According to cooksinfo.com, the word *succotash* comes from the word *msickquatash* used by the Narragansett Indians in Rhode Island. It appears to have meant either "boiled corn kernels" or "broken into bits." Certainly there are so many recipes for succotash that it's hard to claim that there is a definitive recipe. The Southern version uses lima beans, while the New England version calls for cooked dried beans. *The Boston Cooking-School Cook Book* has only the briefest instructions: "Cut hot boiled corn from cob, add equal quantity of hot boiled shell beans; season with salt and pepper and reheat before serving." Venerable *Yankee* magazine's cookbook, *Lost and Vintage Recipes,* elaborates a bit more in the recipe below.

New England Succotash

SERVES 6-8.

> 6 ears fresh corn
>
> 4 tablespoons unsalted butter, divided
>
> 3 cups fresh cranberry beans, or fresh or frozen lima beans
>
> ⅛ pound salt pork, cut into 4 pieces (optional)
>
> ½ small onion, minced
>
> 2 teaspoons granulated sugar
>
> Kosher or sea salt and freshly ground black pepper, to taste
>
> ¼ cup heavy cream (optional)

1. Use a sharp knife to cut the kernels off the cobs, and set aside.

2. In a large saucepan over medium heat, melt 1 tablespoon butter. Add the beans, salt pork (if using), and onion. Cook, stirring often, until the beans are tender and the onion is golden, about 10 minutes.

3. Stir in the corn and add enough water to cover by ½ inch. Add the sugar and remaining 3 tablespoons butter. Bring to a gentle bubble and cook, uncovered, for 10 minutes.

4. Remove the salt pork and season the succotash with salt and pepper to taste. Add cream, if desired.

Corn Chowder

There are infinite varieties of farmhouse chowders, but the most traditional of these is corn chowder. This recipe comes from Boston chef Jasper White's chowder treatise, *50 Chowders*.

SERVES 4.

4-ounce slab unsliced bacon, rind removed and cut into ⅓-inch dice

2 tablespoons unsalted butter

1 medium onion (7–8 ounces), cut into ½-inch dice

½ large red bell pepper (6–8 ounces), cut into ½-inch dice

1–2 springs fresh thyme, leaves removed and chopped (about ½ teaspoon fresh or scant ¼ teaspoon dried)

½ teaspoon ground cumin

⅛ teaspoon turmeric

3 medium ears fresh yellow or bicolor corn, husked and cut from cob (or substitute 2 cups frozen kernels)

1 pound Yukon gold, Maine, Prince Edward Island, or other all-purpose potatoes, peeled and cut into ½-inch dice

3 cups chicken stock

Kosher or sea salt and freshly ground black pepper

2 teaspoons cornstarch

2 tablespoons water

1 cup cream

2 tablespoons minced fresh chives or thinly sliced scallions (for garnish)

1. Heat a 3- to 4-quart heavy pot over low heat and add the diced bacon. Once it has rendered a few tablespoons of fat, increase the heat to medium, and cook until the bacon is crisp and golden brown. Pour off all but 1 tablespoon bacon fat, leaving the bacon in the pot.

2. Add the butter, onion, bell pepper, thyme, cumin, and turmeric; sauté, stirring occasionally with a wooden spoon, for about 8 minutes, until the onion and pepper are tender but not browned.

3. Add the corn kernels, potatoes, and stock. Turn up the heat, cover, and boil vigorously for about 10 minutes. Some of the potatoes will have broken up, but most should retain their shape. Use the back of your spoon to smash a bit of the corn and potatoes against the side of the pot. Reduce the heat to medium and season the chowder with salt and pepper.

4. Dissolve the cornstarch in the water and slowly pour it into the pot, stirring constantly. As soon as the chowder has come back to a boil and thickened slightly, remove the pot from the heat and stir in the cream. Adjust the seasoning if necessary. If you are not serving the chowder within the hour, let it cool a bit, then refrigerate. Cover the chowder after it has chilled completely. Otherwise, let it sit at room temperature for up to an hour, allowing the flavors to meld.

5. When ready to serve, reheat the chowder over low heat. Don't let it boil. Ladle into bowls and sprinkle with chives or scallions.

Chanterelle and Corn Bisque

This recipe comes from one of my favorite people in the culinary world, Evan Mallet, former chef at Lindbergh's Crossing and now owner of the Black Trumpet in Portsmouth, New Hampshire. He has been a James Beard nominee for Best Chef Northeast multiple times. His recent cookbook, *Black Trumpet: A Chef's Journey Through Eight New England Seasons*, is a gem.

SERVES 6.

> 1 leek, white part only, chopped, rinsed well, and drained
>
> 2 carrots, peeled and chopped
>
> 1 red potato, washed and chopped
>
> 1 small celery root bulb, peeled and diced
>
> 2 ears corn, shucked, kernels cut from the cob
>
> ½ pound chanterelles, brushed and chopped
>
> Salt, to taste
>
> Pinch of nutmeg
>
> Pinch of white pepper
>
> Pinch of cayenne
>
> 2 tablespoons tomato paste
>
> 1 cup sherry (dry or medium-dry)
>
> 2 cups half-and-half
>
> 2 cups chicken or vegetable stock
>
> 1 tablespoon chopped fresh thyme
>
> 1 bay leaf
>
> 1 tablespoon sea salt

1. In a medium stock pot over low heat, sauté the leeks, carrots, potato, celery, corn, and mushrooms with a little salt until they start to stick to the bottom of the pot.

2. Stir in the nutmeg, white pepper, cayenne, and tomato paste. Deglaze the pot with sherry and simmer until the veggies are sticking again. Pour in the half-and-half while stirring briskly. Continue stirring and add the stock, thyme, bay leaf, and salt.

3. Simmer for about 20 minutes. Serve hot, or make a day ahead, cool down in ice water, and reserve in the fridge. For a special treat, add some cooked lobster meat to the final product.

Pumpkins and Squash

"I would rather sit on a pumpkin and have it all to myself, than be crowded on a velvet cushion."

—Henry David Thoreau

Pumpkins and squash are synonymous with autumn in New England. They are (and were) widely available, pack a nutritional punch, and keep extremely well in the colder months (though there is a squirrel that likes to nosh on our porch pumpkin). Squashes, to my mind, are interchangeable with pie or sugar pumpkins as opposed to the large jack-o-lantern type. When roasted, they may have a creamier texture.

Broiled Butternut Squash with Apples

SERVES 6-8.

2 pounds butternut squash, peeled, cut lengthwise in half, seeded, and cut into ½-inch pieces

3 tablespoons extra-virgin olive oil, divided

Maldon or other flaky sea salt and coarsely ground black pepper

2 medium Granny Smith apples, peeled, quartered, cored, and cut into ½-inch pieces

1 cup apple cider

2 tablespoons lower sodium soy sauce

2 tablespoons sherry vinegar

2 tablespoons finely chopped fresh sage

1. Preheat the broiler. Toss the squash with 2 tablespoons of the oil in a large bowl and season with salt and pepper. Spread the squash out on a baking sheet in a single layer (set the bowl aside) and broil, stirring occasionally, until lightly charred in spots and beginning to soften, about 10 minutes. Toss the apples with the remaining 1 tablespoon oil and season with salt and pepper. Toss with the squash on the baking sheet and broil, stirring occasionally, until the squash and apples are tender. Return to the bowl.

2. Meanwhile, bring the cider to a boil in a small saucepan, and boil until it is syrupy and reduced to 2 tablespoons. Remove from the heat.

3. Combine the reduced cider, soy sauce, vinegar, and sage in a small bowl and whisk well. Pour over the squash and apples, tossing to coat. Serve, or let stand at room temperature for 1 hour to bring out the flavors. (The squash and apples can be refrigerated for up to 3 days; bring to room temperature before serving.)

Roasted Pumpkin and Bean Spread

MAKES 2-3 CUPS.

¼ cup extra-virgin olive oil, plus enough to coat pan

1 (3–4 pound) pumpkin, cut in half and seeds scooped out

½ pound Great Northern beans

Salt and pepper, to taste

1 cup pumpkin seeds, roasted and finely chopped

2 tablespoons fresh lemon juice

1 tablespoon curry powder

1 tablespoon cider molasses

1. Preheat the oven to 325°F.

2. Lightly coat a sheet pan with oil. Place pumpkin cut-side down on pan, and roast until tender, about 1 to 1¼ hours. Set aside and scoop out when cool enough to handle.

3. Place the beans in a pot with enough water to cover by a few inches. Simmer until tender, about an hour. Season lightly with salt and pepper. Drain and reserve ½ cup of broth. Let the pumpkin and beans cool.

4. Using an immersion blender (or a food processor and working in two batches), puree the pumpkin, beans, seeds, lemon juice, curry, molasses, and olive oil. Add salt and pepper to taste (if mixture is too thick, add reserved bean broth). Great as a dip or a sandwich spread for pork, turkey, or vegetables.

Butternut Squash Custard

I love winter squash in just about any form, but this recipe amps up the flavor while enhancing the texture. (Plus it looks nice.)

SERVES 8 AS A SIDE DISH.

3 pounds peeled butternut squash cut into 1-inch chunks

Salt, to taste

½ cup butter, softened

¼ cup sugar

½ teaspoon baking powder

½ teaspoon nutmeg

1 teaspoon salt

¼ cup flour

4 eggs

1. Preheat the oven to 400°F.

2. Cook the squash 15-20 minutes until very tender, in enough water to cover with a pinch or two of salt; mash well.

3. Beat together the squash, butter, sugar, and dry ingredients. Whisk in the eggs for 3 to 4 minutes.

4. Grease a 4-cup soufflé dish or 8 individual ramekins. Pour in the squash mixture.

5. Bake for 50 minutes, until slightly puffed and golden on top.

Fried Parsnip Fritters

This comes from *Mrs. Lincoln's Boston Cook Book,* by Mary Johnson Bailey Lincoln, 1884.

Batter

Yolks of two eggs, beaten well; add half a cup of milk or water, and one tablespoon of olive oil, one spoonful of salt, and one cup of flour, or enough to make it almost a drop batter. When ready to use, add the whites of the eggs, beaten very stiff. Parsnips should be boiled till tender, then drained and cut into small pieces; then stir them into the fritter batter.

On Frying...

The fat should be clean, new fat, half-lard and half-clarified beef drippings. By new fat is meant that it has not been used for meat or fish or become browned by previous frying. The same fat may be used several times by clarifying with several thin slices of raw potato and straining through a fine strainer after each frying.

It should be very hot and still, not bubbling, but not as hot as for mixtures which have been previously cooked. The surest way is to fry a bit of the mixture. It should rise at once to the surface, with much sputtering of the fat, swell, and begin to brown on the under side. Fritters should be turned. They should be cooked an even golden brown and the fat kept at the right temperature by moving the kettle farther from or nearer to the fire. Try them with a fork, and if it comes out clean, they are done.

Drain each cake fritter over the hot fat, and when they cease to drip, put them in a strainer placed in a pan on the back of the stove or drain on soft brown paper. Change the first cooked to another pan when the next are ready to be taken out.

Pickles and Preserves

Both pickling and preserving are ways of keeping fruit and vegetables on hand throughout the winter. "Putting up" was a necessary activity when harvest time came around. Many an early New Englander would rely on these (along with other methods like smoking, curing, and salting for fish and meat) to feed their families.

Bread and Butter Pickles

Cucumbers are abundant in early fall, so take advantage and use the freshest cukes possible. Make these to eat just for the week or preserve for the weeks to come.

MAKES 4 PINTS.

2½ pounds farm-fresh pickling cucumbers

1 pound white or yellow onions, thinly sliced

¼ cup pickling salt

1¼ cups white distilled vinegar (5% acidity)

1 cup apple cider vinegar (5% acidity)

2¼ cups sugar

1 tablespoon mustard seeds

Pinch of crushed red pepper flakes (optional)

1 cinnamon stick

6 whole cloves plus a pinch of ground cloves

½ teaspoon turmeric

1. Rinse the cucumbers and scrub off any dirt. Slice off ⅛-inch from the ends and discard. Slice the cucumbers in ¼-inch-thick slices and place in a large bowl. Add the sliced onions and pickling salt. Stir in so that the salt is well distributed among the cucumber slices. Cover with a clean, thin towel. Cover with a couple inches of ice. Put in the refrigerator and let chill for 4 hours. Discard ice. Rinse the cucumber and onion slices thoroughly and drain. Rinse and drain again.

2. If you plan to store your pickles outside of the refrigerator for any length of time, you will need to sterilize your jars before canning, and heat the filled jars in a hot-water bath after canning. If you are eating the pickles right away, skip the water bath step. To sterilize the jars for canning, place empty jars on a metal rack in a large, 16-quart canning pot. Fill with warm water and bring to a boil. Reduce heat to warm to keep the jars hot and ready for filling. Remove with tongs or jar lifters one by one as you can the cucumbers. Sterilize the lids by bringing a pot of water to a boil and pouring water into a bowl containing the lids.

3. In a 6-quart pot, place the vinegars, sugar, and all of the spices. Bring to a boil. Once the sugar has dissolved, add the sliced cucumbers and onions. Bring to a boil again. As soon as the sugar and vinegar solution begins boiling again, use a slotted spoon to start packing the hot jars with the cucumbers. Pack a jar to an inch from the rim with the vegetables. Pour hot vinegar sugar syrup over the vegetables to ½-inch from the rim. Wipe the rim clean with a paper towel. Place a sterilized lid on the jar. Secure with a metal screw band top.

4. If you are planning to store pickles outside of the refrigerator, process the filled jars in a hot-water bath for 10 minutes. Return the filled jars to the same canning pot with its already hot water. The water level needs to be at least 1 inch above the top of the pickles. Bring to a boil and let boil hard for 15 minutes, or 20 minutes for altitudes of 1,001 to 6,000 feet. Over 6,000 feet, boil for 25 minutes. Remove the jars from the pot. Let the jars cool down to room temperature. The jars should make a popping sound as their lids seal.

Pickled Green Beans

In New England, dilly beans are a ubiquitous country store treat. Judith Choate, who provided this recipe, is a chef, cookbook author, consultant, and recipe developer, with both James Beard and IACP awards to her credit. She has authored or co-authored more than one hundred books. For more of her recipes, visit www.judithchoate.com.

MAKES ABOUT THREE 4-OUNCE JARS.

2 pounds very fresh green beans (preferably organic) or *haricots vert*, stem end removed, well-washed

1 cup white vinegar

¼ cup water

¼ cup sugar

2 teaspoons mustard seeds

1 teaspoon celery seed

1 teaspoon dried red chili flakes or to taste

½ teaspoon coarse salt

1 tablespoon chopped fresh dill

6 whole peeled garlic cloves

3 sprigs fresh dill

1. Place the beans in a large pot of cold salted water. Place over medium-high heat and bring to a boil. Lower the heat and simmer for about 4 minutes or until crisp-tender. Immediately remove from the heat, drain well, and place in a bowl of ice water to stop the cooking and set the color. When cool, remove from the ice water and pat very dry. Set aside.

2. Combine the vinegar, water, sugar, mustard seeds, celery seeds, chili flakes, and salt in a medium nonreactive pan over high heat. Bring to a boil; then, lower the heat and simmer for 5 minutes. Remove from the heat and stir in the chopped dill.

3. Fit the beans into the jars, vertically. Add 2 garlic cloves and 1 sprig of dill to each jar. Pour the hot vinegar solution into each jar, covering the beans completely while leaving about ¼ inch of headroom. If you do not plan long storage, the beans may be cooled and stored in the refrigerator for up to a month or so.

Note: If longer storage is desired, place the jars in a large pot or canner with a rack placed in the bottom. Cover with cold water by at least 2 inches and place over high heat. Cover and bring to a boil. Boil, covered, for 10 minutes. Using tongs, remove the jars from the canner and set aside on a wire rack to cool before storing. Beans may be stored for up to 1 year, but are best served within 6 months.

Fowl

"To the avid water fowler, no moment of truth can match the instant when a flock first responds to his call and decoys, the time when this wild, free bird of unsurpassed grace begins a descent from the sky down to gun range. It is a stirring spectacle."

—Grits Gresham, *The Complete Wildfowler*

Although we now have the convenience of buying our fowl from the store or butcher shop, as many people would have in the 1800s, there are avid bird hunters to this day, though wild specimens are often less tender than their farm-raised kin. Brining is a good way to tenderize and add moisture.

Honey-Glazed Duck

This recipe, which makes use of two ingredients originally gathered and hunted, comes from *The Backyard Beekeeper's Honey Handbook* by Kim Flottum.

SERVES 2 TO 4.

1 (5-pound) duckling
½ cup honey (use a mild but flavorful variety)
½ teaspoon garlic salt
½ teaspoon onion salt
1 teaspoon poultry seasoning
½ teaspoon paprika
1 teaspoon salt
½ cup orange juice with pulp
1½ teaspoons mustard powder
5–6 very thin orange slices
5–6 very thin onion slices

1. Preheat the oven to 450°F. Remove any pinfeathers from the duck, and clean it inside and out. Prick the skin so the fat can easily drain from the meat.

2. In a small bowl, combine the honey, garlic salt, onion salt, poultry seasoning, paprika, and salt. Rub all over the inside and outside of the duck.

3. Place in a shallow baking pan and bake for 15 minutes. Quickly remove, reduce the oven to 350°F, and drain the fat from the pan.

4. Return the pan to the oven and bake for 1 hour, draining the fat as needed. Meanwhile, combine the orange juice and mustard.

5. After 1 hour, remove the duck and brush with some of the orange juice mixture. Using toothpicks, cover the duck with the orange and onion slices.

6. Return to the oven for another 45 minutes, brushing occasionally with the orange juice mixture. Let stand for at least 15 minutes before cutting and serving.

Jacques Pepin's Duck Giblet Salad

This recipe comes from Judith Jones's memoir *The Tenth Muse*. Jones was one of the culinary and literary powerhouses of our time. She was the editor at Knopf who championed the publication of Julia Child's *Mastering the Art of French Cooking* as well as *The Diary of Anne Frank*. I had the great pleasure of meeting her, and on another occasion, dining with Jacques Pepin and his wife.

As Jones says in her memoir, "I consider one of the best cook's treats the packet of giblets that one finds tucked into a roasting bird—and if you don't find it, complain loudly and never buy from that source again. So I was delighted at Jacques's recipe for a duck giblet salad. He says it will serve two, but I found it so good that I ate the whole thing."

SERVES 1–2.

Giblets

1 packet duck giblets (gizzard, heart, and liver)

2 tablespoons butter

2 teaspoons duck fat

Salt and freshly ground pepper

Dressing

½ teaspoon salt

1 shallot, finely chopped

2 teaspoons Dijon mustard

1 tablespoon red wine vinegar

1 tablespoon duck fat

1½ tablespoons olive oil

Escarole, endive, watercress, or any mix of more assertive salad greens

1 tablespoon duck cracklings (duck skin rendered and slowly cooked until crunchy)

1. Trim the membrane from the side of the gizzard, and slice it and the heart into thin strips. After discarding any fat and membrane from the liver, cut it up into somewhat thicker pieces.

2. Melt the butter and duck fat in a small skillet, and sauté the gizzard and heart strips over medium-high heat for about 2½ minutes, tossing frequently and adding the liver for the final minute. Salt and pepper the meats, and remove them from the pan.

3. For the dressing, mix together the salt, shallot, mustard, vinegar, duck fat, and olive oil, then pour it into the pan and scrape up all the juices.

4. Heap the greens onto a plate or bowl, and toss with a couple tablespoons of the dressing.

5. Mix the giblets with most of the remaining dressing, taste, and arrange them on top of the greens. Toss cracklings over all.

Grilled Quail

While quail is a small bird, usually less than 8 ounces, it is still a prized morsel at the table. Although this recipe calls for ingredients that might have been difficult to find back in the day, it's a simple recipe for today's home cooks.

SERVES 4 AS A MAIN COURSE OR 8 AS AN APPETIZER.

¼ cup Dijon mustard

¼ cup brown sugar

1 tablespoon kosher salt

2 tablespoons minced fresh thyme

½ cup thinly sliced shallots

2 tablespoons thinly sliced garlic

2 tablespoons orange zest

2 tablespoons lemon zest

½ cup olive oil

8 quail, spatchcocked (instructions below)

Freshly cracked black pepper

1 lemon, halved

1. In a large bowl, combine the Dijon mustard, brown sugar, salt, thyme, shallots, garlic, orange zest, lemon zest, and olive oil. Add the quail to the bowl and gently toss, making sure each quail is completely coated in the marinade. Marinate for at least 1 hour, and no more than 6 hours.

2. Turn the grill on and let it heat to medium-high. Lay the quail on a sheet pan. Squeeze all over with one-half of the lemon and sprinkle with the desired amount of cracked pepper. Flip over and repeat with the remaining lemon and cracked pepper.

3. Grill 4 or 5 minutes per side, until just cooked through.

To Spatchcock Quail

1. Cut the wing tips off of the quail (wing tips and all other bones can be reserved for stock).
2. Lay the quail breast-side down on a cutting board. Using sharp kitchen shears, cut along either side of the backbone until the backbone is removed from the body of the quail (save the bones for stock).
3. Lay the bird open, still breast-side down, and gently press to flatten. Remove the small rib bones with your fingers (they should pull away from the meat pretty easily).
4. Slide your finger along either side of the breastbone and then wiggle the breastbone free from the bird. Using a mallet, gently pound the breasts one or two times to slightly flatten.

Roast Goose with Sherry-Orange Glaze

I once prepared this dish at a cooking class/demo, and although it was indeed delicious, the cost of my meaty, specially ordered goose was a bit prohibitive. But when you want to pull out all the stops for a holiday or special occasion meal, there are few birds more impressive. The traditional English holiday stuffing for roast goose is a sage and onion mixture. A mixture of apples and peeled chestnuts is wonderful, too.

SERVES 6-8.

> 1 (10- to 12-pound) whole goose, giblets removed
>
> Juice of 1 orange, rind reserved
>
> Coarse salt and coarsely ground black pepper
>
> 8 slices bacon
>
> 1 cup chicken broth
>
> ½ cup medium sherry
>
> 1 tablespoon orange marmalade
>
> 1 tablespoon butter

1. Preheat the oven to 325°F. Rinse the goose thoroughly inside and out, and pat dry. Prick the skin all over with a fork. Rub inside and out with the orange rind, then season inside and out with the salt and pepper.

2. Stuff the goose with your favorite stuffing, and close with poultry lacing skewers.

3. Place the goose, breast-side up, on a rack in a large roasting pan. Lay the bacon slices across the breast. Roast the goose for 1½ hours, removing fat from the pan every 30 minutes.

4. Remove the bacon strips. Continue to roast the goose until a meat thermometer inserted deep into the thigh reads between 175°F and 180°F (about 3 hours), again spooning off excess fat occasionally. Transfer the goose to a platter, cover loosely with aluminum foil, and let rest for 20 minutes.

5. Pour off any remaining fat from the roasting pan. Add the chicken broth, orange juice, and sherry to the pan and bring to a boil, scraping any browned bits from the bottom of the pan. Simmer over low heat for 5 minutes. Add the marmalade and simmer, stirring constantly, for 2 minutes.

6. Just before carving the goose, finish the pan gravy by warming the broth mixture over low heat. Whisk in the butter until the sauce is melted and velvety. Serve hot with the carved goose.

Roasted Heritage Turkey

A free-range heritage turkey will be leaner and have more muscle than a commercially raised turkey and therefore will require a bit more cooking time. Again, brining the bird can improve texture.

SERVES 6–8.

> 1 (10- to 15-pound) heritage turkey
>
> 1¼ teaspoons salt, divided
>
> ¾ teaspoon freshly ground pepper, divided
>
> 1 medium onion, diced
>
> 2 tablespoons rosemary
>
> 2 tablespoons sage
>
> ¼ cup melted butter
>
> 1½ cups water

1. Preheat the oven to 325°F.

2. Rinse the turkey well with cold running water, both inside and out. Pat dry inside and out. Rub the inside of the turkey with a mixture of ¾ teaspoon salt and ¼ teaspoon freshly ground pepper. Add the diced onion and herbs to the cavity. Use skewers to pin the neck skin to the underside of the bird, and fold the wings behind the back. Next, tie the drumsticks together to reduce cavity space.

3. Rub the entire turkey with butter. Sprinkle ½ teaspoon salt and ½ teaspoon freshly ground pepper on the outside of the turkey. Place the turkey on a rack in a large roasting pan. Add the water to the bottom of the pan. Place in the oven for 30 minutes. Remove from the oven, and baste the exterior with natural juices and melted butter from the pan. Cover tightly and return to the oven. Continue to bake for 15 to 20 minutes per pound.

To check doneness, the drumsticks will feel tender when pressed, and juices from the turkey will run clear. If using a meat thermometer, insert it into the inner thigh area, near the breast, but not touching the bone. It should reach 180°F.

4. Thirty minutes before turkey is done, remove the cover, and baste with the juice and butter mixture from the pan. Return to the oven in open roasting pan to brown lightly. Allow to rest for 20 minutes before carving.

Meat and Game

"The old man used to say that the best part of hunting and fishing was the thinking about going and the talking about it after you got back."

—Robert Ruark, *The Old Man and the Boy*

There would have been all sorts of animals hunted for their meat in the early days. Cattle and sheep arrived from Old World sources and were soon a staple. One thing we know for sure is that settlers and Native Americans both ate a much wider variety of game than we could imagine now. An exception to that might be my friend Kate Krukowski Gooding, hunter, chef, and author of *Black Fly Stew* (and other fun and original titles), who hunts moose, bear, and beaver to name a few.

Even the 1973 edition of *Joy of Cooking* includes preparation guidelines for squirrel, opossum, porcupine, raccoons, muskrat, and woodchuck.

In addition, many more parts of any animal would have been included on the menu. Happily, today's chefs are embracing using the whole beast, right down to pigs' feet and marrow bones. The 1896 *Boston Cooking-School Cook Book* describes "Other Parts of Beef Creature Used for Food." Included are brains, tongue, heart, liver, kidneys, tail, suet, and tripe, along with the best methods for preparation.

Venison Meatloaf

There is good evidence that venison was the main course at the feast thought to have inspired the first Thanksgiving. Massasoit and his Wampanoag tribesmen delivered five deer for the feast, which took place in 1621. This is a family recipe that has a permanent place in my recipe box.

SERVES 4-6.

> 2 eggs
> 1 (14.5 oz) can tomato sauce
> 1 medium onion, chopped
> 1 cup dry bread crumbs
> 1½ teaspoons salt
> Freshly ground pepper to taste
> 1½ pounds ground venison
> 2 tablespoons brown sugar
> 2 tablespoons cider vinegar
> 2 tablespoons spicy brown mustard

1. Beat the eggs and add the tomato sauce, onion, and bread crumbs. Combine well and add salt and pepper.

2. Add the venison and mix well. (Clean hands work well here.)

3. Combine the brown sugar, vinegar, and mustard. Spread over the meat loaf and bake at 350°F for 45 minutes, or until a meat thermometer reads 160°F.

Hunter's Pie

Taste of Home magazine first published this rich recipe in 1997 under the name Colonial Game Pie. It may be vintage but probably not colonial, as the first commercial canning operation in the United States was started in 1813 and the recipe calls for canned goods.

SERVES 16.

½ pound sliced bacon, diced

2½ pounds beef stew meat, cubed

2 (14½-ounce) cans beef broth

½ cup red currant jelly

2 (3-pound) dressed rabbits, cut up

1 (14½-ounce) can chicken broth

¼ cup Worcestershire sauce

1 bay leaf

1 teaspoon salt

¼ teaspoon pepper

¼ teaspoon cayenne pepper

¼ pound pearl onions

2 medium carrots, diced

2 medium potatoes, diced

½ cup fresh mushrooms

1 dressed duck (about 4½ pounds), cut into pieces

6 tablespoons flour

¾ cup water

1 (17¼ ounce) carton of puff pastry

1. In a Dutch oven, cook the bacon until crisp. Drain, reserving the bacon and ¼ cup drippings in the pan. Brown the beef in the drippings. Add the beef broth and jelly; cover and simmer 45 minutes.

2. Cover the rabbits with water in a stockpot or Dutch oven; simmer for 1 hour, or until the meat falls from the bones. Remove the meat and set aside (discard the bones).

3. To the beef mixture, add the chicken broth, Worcestershire, bay leaf, salt, pepper, and cayenne; simmer 20 minutes. Add the onions, carrots, potatoes, and mushrooms; simmer 20 minutes, or until tender. Remove the bay leaf.

4. In another pot, cover the duck with water; simmer until the meat nearly falls from the bones, about 35-45 minutes. Remove the meat and set aside. Mix the flour and water and stir it into the beef mixture. Cook until thickened. Add the rabbit and duck meat.

5. Preheat the oven to 400°F. Cut the puff pastry into 3-inch squares and place them on a greased baking sheet. Bake for 10 to 12 minutes; place on individual servings of meat mixture.

Slow-Braised Pork Roast with Roasted Root Vegetables

Hunting was an essential part of putting food on the table in New England until relatively recently. Especially during lean times, game was a tremendous source of protein, and wild boar was a delicious (if dangerous) quarry. There are still game preserves where wild boar can be hunted. Luckily, farm-raised pork is readily available. The loin is a great economical cut of meat but can be quite dry if overcooked. I cook this often at our local soup kitchen, and braising or stuffing the loin is a good way to go.

SERVES 6-8.

2 tablespoons all-purpose flour

Kosher salt and freshly ground black pepper

1 (3-pound) pork loin

¼ cup canola oil

2 tablespoons Dijon mustard

2 tablespoons whole-grain mustard

1 cup white wine

2 cups chicken stock

1 tablespoon kosher salt

10 peppercorns

6 sprigs rosemary

2 medium turnips, peeled and cut into 1-inch wedges

3 medium yellow beets, peeled and cut into 1-inch wedges

18 large pearl onions, peeled

6 small parsnips, peeled and cut into 1-inch pieces

3 tablespoons unsalted butter

1. Preheat the oven to 400°F. Combine the flour, salt, and pepper to taste and coat the pork loin with it. Heat the oil in an ovenproof casserole or Dutch oven over medium-high heat. Brown the loin on all sides.

2. Using a spatula, coat the loin with the mustards. Add the white wine and chicken stock, salt, peppercorns, and rosemary. Add all of the vegetables. Cover the casserole and place in the oven. After 40 minutes, remove the parsnips, turnips, and onions and set aside, keeping them warm. Turn the loin over and continue cooking for 30 minutes.

3. Remove the beets and keep them warm. Turn the loin over again. Cook until the internal temperature is 140°F to 145°F for medium. Remove the loin from the pan. Pour the liquid through a sieve and return the liquid to the casserole. Place the vegetables on a serving plate. Slice the pork. Whisk the butter in the liquid and pour over the loin. Serve at once.

Corned Beef

The much-maligned New England Boiled Dinner is really quite delicious, especially if you "corn" your own, avoiding the additives in most store-bought corned beef and creating a spice mixture to suit your own tastes. Double your spice blend, omitting additional salt, so you can cook the corned beef in the same seasonings in which it's been brined.

SERVES 8.

4 pounds beef brisket	1 teaspoon mustard seeds
¼ cup salt	4 whole cloves
Water to cover	1 teaspoon black peppercorns
3 cups sea salt or kosher salt	8 whole allspice berries
½ cup sugar	3 garlic cloves, minced
4 bay leaves	2 quarts water

1. Trim all but ¼ inch of fat from the meat. Wash and pat dry. Rub with ¼ cup salt.

2. In a large saucepan, heat the water, salt, and sugar and stir to dissolve. Add the herbs and spices. Place the beef in a large nonreactive bowl and pour the salted water mixture over the top.

3. Place a weighted plate over the meat so it is completely immersed. Refrigerate 4 to 5 days.

4. Remove the meat and rinse thoroughly. Place in a large saucepan and cover with the water. Cover and simmer for 3 to 4 hours, or until the meat is tender.

Note: For a boiled dinner, add your favorite root veggies near the end of cooking, or spoon cooking liquid into another pot and simmer until cooked through. If using turnips, carrots, and/or beets, scrub them, cut into chunks, and allow enough time for them to cook through but not get mushy. Cut the potatoes into similar-sized chunks, and cut cabbage into wedges and cook just until tender.

Corned Beef Hash

The word *hash* comes from the French *hacher*, meaning "to slice or chop up." The dish, at least in this country, is better known as the king of leftovers. The argument could be made that the best reason for making a corned beef dinner is so that you can make hash the next day.

SERVES 4–6.

> 3 tablespoons unsalted butter
>
> 1 cup finely chopped red bell pepper
>
> 2 cloves garlic minced
>
> 5 cups corned beef and potatoes, well drained and chopped
>
> ½ teaspoon chopped fresh thyme
>
> ½ teaspoon chopped fresh oregano
>
> ¼ teaspoon freshly ground black pepper

1. Melt the butter in a 12-inch cast-iron skillet over medium heat. Add the bell pepper and cook until it begins to brown, 5 to 6 minutes.

2. Add the garlic, corned beef and potatoes, thyme, oregano, and black pepper to the skillet and stir to combine. Then spread the hash evenly over the bottom of the skillet.

3. Place a lid from a narrower pan, a heatproof plate, or a second pan directly atop the hash and mash down lightly. Leave the lid in place and cook for 10 to 12 minutes, until browned.

4. Stir up the hash, then mash again. Cook, with the lid in place, for another 5 to 10 minutes, until browned. Serve immediately.

Breads and Baked Goods

"We must have a pie. Stress cannot exist in the presence of a pie."

—David Mamet

Anadama Bread

Anadama bread is a great example of how recipes evolved after New Englanders were introduced to "Indian meal." The stories about how this bread got its name sound like folklore to me, but it's usually about a woman named Anna and someone, her husband perhaps, saying, "Anna, dam her!" Then the husband proceeds to come up with this New England classic. Hmm.

MAKES 1 SANDWICH LOAF OR 2 HALF LOAVES.

¾ cup yellow cornmeal

1¼ teaspoons salt

3 tablespoons butter

¼ cup dark molasses

1 cup boiling water

¼ cup nonfat dry milk

2 cups unbleached all-purpose flour

1 cup white whole wheat flour*

2½ teaspoons instant yeast

Some variations of this bread include rye flour. Substitute ½ cup white rye flour for ½ cup whole wheat flour, if desired.

1. Whisk together the cornmeal and salt. Add the butter and molasses to the bowl.

2. Pour in the boiling water, stirring until the butter has melted and the mixture is smooth. Let the mixture cool to lukewarm, about 15 minutes.

3. Mix in the dry milk, flours, and yeast. Let the dough rest for 20 minutes; this gives the flours and cornmeal a chance to absorb the liquid.

4. Knead the dough for about 7 minutes at medium speed in a stand mixer (or by hand) until it's smooth. It'll be quite stiff but still fairly sticky on the surface. Cover the bowl, and let the dough rise until it's just about doubled, about 1 hour.

5. Gently deflate the dough, and shape it into an 8-inch log. Place the log in an 8½ x 4½-inch loaf pan, cover the pan, and let the dough rise until the center has crested at least 1 inch above the lip of the pan, about 90 minutes.

6. Toward the end of the rising time, preheat the oven to 350°F.

7. Bake the bread for 35 to 40 minutes, until an instant-read thermometer inserted into the center registers at least 190°F. You may want to tent the bread loosely with aluminum foil for the final 15 minutes of baking, if you prefer a lighter crust.

Corn Bread

Corn bread is believed to be one of the original American dishes. It's likely that Native Americans had been making similar dishes long before the first settlers arrived. The corn they grew was not sweet corn, but a hard corn that was ground into meal and used in many dishes. There are cornbread variations from region to region, and it's also known as Johnny Cake. As early as 1787, the author of *The Compleat American Housewife* says, "Our citizens both high and low, mean and genteel, love Johnny Cake." This recipe comes from the iconic Union Oyster House in Boston, Massachusetts, the oldest restaurant in the country.

SERVES 8-10.

¾ cup butter, softened

2 cups sugar

2 tablespoons baking powder

2 teaspoons salt

3 eggs

½ cup vegetable oil

1 cup cornmeal

3¼ cups flour

2 cups milk

1. Preheat the oven to 350°F. Grease and flour a 9 x 13-inch baking dish. In a mixing bowl, cream together the butter, sugar, baking powder, and salt. Add the eggs, one at a time, beating well after each addition.

2. Add the oil and cornmeal, and mix for about 30 seconds. Scrape the sides of the bowl and beat about 15 seconds more.

3. Add the flour, and mix. Add the milk and beat until smooth.

4. Pour the batter into the pan and bake for 30 to 35 minutes, or until a toothpick inserted into the center comes out clean.

Parker House Rolls

These have been a staple of our Thanksgiving table for many years. None other than James Beard himself described their origins. "Parker House rolls . . . were created, so the story goes, by the Parker House in Boston, which was one of our great nineteenth-century hostelries. Some versions are exceedingly good and some are absolutely dreadful because they skimp on good ingredients. Parker House rolls should be delicate, soft, and rather sweet, typical of American rolls in the nineteenth century, and they consume butter by the tons."

MAKES 30-36 ROLLS.

> 2 packages active dry yeast
>
> 1 tablespoon granulated sugar
>
> ½ cup warm water (100ºF–115ºF, approximately)
>
> ½ stick (¼ cup) butter, cut into small pieces
>
> 2 cups warm milk
>
> 5–6 cups all-purpose flour
>
> 2 teaspoons salt
>
> ¼–½ cup melted butter
>
> 1 egg, beaten with 2 tablespoons light cream or milk

1. Dissolve the yeast and the sugar in the warm water and allow to proof. Melt the half stick of butter in the warm milk, then combine with the yeast mixture in a large mixing bowl. Mix 2 to 3 cups of flour with the salt and stir, 1 cup at a time, into the mixture in the bowl, beating vigorously with a wooden spoon to make a soft sponge. (The dough will be wet and sticky.)

2. Cover the bowl with plastic wrap, set in a warm place, and let the dough rise till doubled in bulk, about 1 hour. Stir it down with a wooden spoon and add about 2 more cups of flour, 1 cup at a time, to make a dough that can be kneaded with ease.

3. Turn out on a lightly floured board and knead until velvety smooth and very elastic; press with the fingers to see if the dough is resilient. Let rest for a few minutes, then form the dough into a ball. Put into a buttered bowl and turn so that the surface is thoroughly covered with butter. Cover and put in a warm, draft-free place to rise again until doubled in bulk.

4. Punch the dough down with your fist, turn out on a lightly floured board, and let rest for several minutes, until you are able to roll it out to a thickness of ½ inch. Cut out rounds of dough with a round 3-inch cutter, or with a water glass dipped in flour. (The odd bits of leftover dough can be reworked into a ball, rolled out, and cut.) Brush the center of each round with melted butter.

5. Take a pencil, a chopstick, or any cylinder of similar size and make a deep indentation in the center of the circle, without breaking through the dough. Fold over one-third of each round and press down to seal.

6. Arrange these folded rolls on a buttered baking sheet about ½ inch apart. Brush again with melted butter and allow the rolls to rise until almost doubled in size. They will probably touch each other. Brush them with the egg wash and bake in a preheated 375ºF oven until lightly browned, about 20 minutes, depending on size. Test one by gently tapping it on the top. If done, you will hear a very faint hollow sound. Or take one, break it open carefully, and see if it is cooked inside.

7. Remove the rolls to a cooling rack and serve piping hot right from the oven, with plenty of butter and preserves or honey, if desired.

Steamed Brown Bread

This New England classic is traditionally served with baked beans. This recipe comes from one of the vessels in the Maine schooner fleet, the *Grace Bailey*, originally a hardworking, cargo-carrying coasting schooner. The *Grace Bailey* was built in 1882 and is now one of only four surviving historic coasters.

MAKES 1 LOAF.

>1 cup boiling water
>⅓ cup raisins (optional)
>⅓ cup cornmeal
>⅓ cup flour
>⅓ cup whole-wheat flour
>¾ teaspoon baking soda
>½ teaspoon salt
>⅔ cup buttermilk
>¼ cup molasses

1. Grease a 1-pound metal coffee can. In a small bowl, pour the boiling water over the raisins, if using. Let stand for 5 minutes or so until they are plumped. Drain and set aside.

2. In a large bowl, whisk together the dry ingredients. Stir in the buttermilk and molasses and beat until smooth. If using the raisins, add them to this mixture.

3. Pour the batter into the prepared coffee can and cover tightly with foil. Tie a piece of kitchen twine around the can to secure the foil. Place the can in a deep pot with a tightly fitting lid.

4. Bring a kettle of water to boil and add enough boiling water to the pot to come one-quarter of the way up the can. Cover and steam over low to medium heat for 3 to 4 hours, replenishing water as needed to remain at least one-quarter of the way up the side of the can. (The water should remain at barely a simmer.)

5. When a knife or skewer comes out clean, gently shake the bread out of the can or remove the bottom of the can and push out. Slice into rounds and serve with butter.

Sweets

Early North American Sweeteners

Sweeteners included fruit, molasses, apple cider molasses, honey, and sugar. Sugar cane came to warmer New World climes via traders like the Portuguese, who encountered the plant in parts of southern Asia. Fast-forward thousands of years, and sugar is already considered a colonial staple. Now, unfortunately, cane sugar is often supplanted by high-fructose corn syrup in hundreds of commercial products.

Maple Walnut Pie

Maple syrup, along with maple sugar, are among the great gifts of our land-scape. Not only are sugar maples the bright stars of foliage season, cold nights and warm spring days make the sap start to flow, and buckets appear wherever these trees flourish. The sap—a clear, thin liquid, ever so faintly sweet—is boiled down in a large, flat pan until it's thick and golden, ready to be strained, bot-tled, and paired with all manner of goodies.

SERVES 10.

Crust

1 cup King Arthur Unbleached All-Purpose Flour

¼ teaspoon salt

¼ cup butter

2 tablespoons vegetable shortening

1 teaspoon fresh lemon juice or vinegar

2–2½ tablespoons water

Filling

3 large eggs

1½ cups Grade B pure maple syrup*

2 tablespoons butter, melted and cooled to lukewarm

1 teaspoon vanilla

¼ teaspoon salt

1 heaping cup walnut pieces

*Note: We realize many people can't obtain maple syrup locally, so feel free to substitute supermarket maple-flavored syrup. The flavor won't be exactly the same, but you'll still have a delicious pie.

1. Preheat the oven to 425°F.

2. In a medium-size mixing bowl, whisk together the flour and salt. Using an electric mixer, a pastry blender, fork, or your fingers, cut the butter and shortening into the flour mixture until the fat and flour form a crumbly mixture. Add the lemon juice or vinegar, then sprinkle on just enough water so that you can gather the dough into a cohesive ball.

3. Flatten the ball of dough into a 1-inch-thick circle, and transfer to a well-floured work surface. Roll it into a 12-inch circle, using as few strokes of the rolling pin as possible; the less you fool around with the crust at this point, the more tender it'll be when it's baked.

4. Transfer the dough to a 9-inch pie plate (a giant spatula works great here), and gently fit it to the pan's contours. If you push or stretch the dough too much, it'll shrink when you put it in the oven. Crimp the edges of the crust.

5. Line the crust with parchment or waxed paper and fill it partway with pie weights or dried beans, or set a perforated pie pan onto the crust. Bake the crust for 15 minutes, then transfer it to a cooling rack, remove the pie weights and parchment (or perforated pie pan), and allow it to cool while you prepare the filling. Lower the oven temperature to 375°F.

6. In a large bowl, beat the eggs until well combined, then add the maple syrup in a slow stream, beating all the time. Stir in the melted butter, vanilla, and salt, then the walnuts. Pour the filling into the prepared crust.

7. Bake for 40 to 45 minutes, until it's somewhat puffed, bubbling, and a knife inserted in the center comes out clean. The crust will be a deep, golden brown. Remove the pie from the oven, and let it cool at least 30 minutes before serving (the filling will sink as it cools; that's okay). Serve with whipped cream or vanilla ice cream, if desired.

Apple & Caramel Bread Pudding

SERVES 6–8.

Pudding

4 cups cubed day-old Italian bread or baguette

1 tablespoon butter, more to butter pan

2 apples, peeled and sliced ¼ inch thick

6 whole eggs

¾ cup sugar

¼ teaspoon cinnamon

1 teaspoon vanilla extract

3 cups milk

Caramel Sauce

¾ cup sugar

¼ cup water

½ cup heavy cream

1. Place the bread in a large bowl. Heat the butter in a large skillet over medium-high heat. Add the apples and cook for about 10 minutes, until they are tender and have caramelized a bit (if they are browning too quickly, reduce heat). Add the apples to the bowl with the bread.

2. Whisk together the eggs, sugar, cinnamon, vanilla, and milk until smooth to form a custard. Pour over the bread and apples, toss well, and soak for 1 or 2 hours, until the bread is completely saturated.

3. Preheat the oven to 325°F. Lightly grease an 8 x 8-inch baking pan. Pour the custard into the pan and bake for 40 to 50 minutes, until set. It's fine if the pudding browns a bit on top. Let the pudding sit for about 10 minutes.

4. To make the caramel, place the sugar in a small saucepan. Pour the water evenly over the sugar and let it sit for a few seconds without stirring, until the sugar has absorbed all the water.

5. Place the pot over medium-high heat and bring to a boil without stirring. Reduce the heat slightly and simmer rapidly for several minutes, until the liquid begins to turn amber around the edges. Once the sugar beings to turn amber, stir gently, being careful not to spatter, until it is a deep amber color.

6. Reduce the heat to low and add the cream, being careful to avoid the burst of steam and boiling sauce that will occur when the cream hits the sugar (sugar will seize up a bit). Stir gently for about a minute, until the sugar dissolves into the cream. While the pudding is still quite warm, pour the warm caramel evenly over the top. Serve warm or at room temperature. Caramel can be kept warm for a few minutes over very low heat, or it can be kept at room temperature for several hours and then rewarmed as needed.

Pumpkin Indian Pudding

This recipe from Chef Brandon Blethen, formerly of Robert's Maine Grill in Kittery, Maine, adds another element to a classic. "I like it straight from the oven, in a bowl with a scoop of vanilla ice cream. I added the pumpkin because it contributes both moistness and flavor," he says.

SERVES 8.

- 4 cups whole milk
- ¼ cup butter
- ½ cup white or yellow cornmeal
- 1 cup pumpkin puree (canned is fine)
- 4 eggs
- ¼ cup sugar
- ¾ cup dark molasses
- 1 teaspoon cinnamon
- 1 teaspoon nutmeg
- ¼ teaspoon salt

1. Preheat the oven to 350°F.

2. In a large saucepan, bring the milk and butter to a gentle boil. Slowly whisk in the cornmeal. Simmer for 1 minute. Let cool for 15 minutes.

3. In a large bowl, combine the pumpkin puree, eggs, sugar, molasses, cinnamon, nutmeg, and salt. Pour in the cornmeal mixture and mix until smooth.

4. Pour the pudding into a buttered 9 x 9-inch baking dish. Place the dish in a large roasting pan, and place the pan in the oven. Pour in boiling water so that the water comes a quarter of the way up the sides of the baking dish.

5. Bake for 1 hour. Remove from the oven and serve warm with ice cream or whipped cream.

Pumpkin Whoopie Pies

With the combination of pumpkin and maple syrup in the form of the classic whoopie pie, there could hardly been a more iconic New England recipe (though the Indian Pudding recipe on the previous page could also be a contender). Several New England states lay claim to being the originators of whoopie pies, but so does Pennsylvania. The Maine Whoopie Pie Festival is held each June in Dover-Foxcroft, Maine. I expect it would be a good place to do some "research."

MAKES 6 CAKES.

Cakes

1 stick unsalted butter, at room temperature

1 cup firmly packed light brown sugar

2 large eggs, at room temperature, lightly beaten

1 cup canned pumpkin purée (not pumpkin-pie filling), such as One-Pie brand

2 teaspoons ground cinnamon

2 teaspoons ground ginger

1 teaspoon vanilla extract

1 teaspoon baking powder

1 teaspoon baking soda

¾ teaspoon salt

1⅔ cups all-purpose flour

Filling

8 ounces cream cheese, at room temperature

½ stick unsalted butter, softened

½ teaspoon vanilla extract

2 tablespoons maple syrup

¾ cup powdered sugar

⅛ teaspoon salt

1. Preheat the oven to 350°F, and line two baking sheets with parchment paper.

2. In a large bowl, cream the butter and brown sugar until smooth. Add eggs, pumpkin purée, spices, vanilla, baking powder, baking soda, and salt. Using a rubber spatula, fold in flour until just combined.

3. With an ice-cream scoop, drop 6 generous mounds of batter, spaced evenly, onto each of two baking sheets to make 12 cakes. Bake until springy to the touch, about 10 minutes. Transfer to a rack to cool completely.

4. To make the filling, in the bowl of a standing mixer or with an electric beater, cream together the cream cheese and butter. Add the vanilla, maple syrup, powdered sugar, and salt.

5. Mix on low speed until blended; then beat on medium-high speed until fluffy, about 2 minutes. Spread the flat sides of six of the cakes with cream-cheese frosting. Top each with another cake and serve or chill.

PHOTO CREDITS

Page 107 © iStock.com/-Ivinst-

Page 112 © iStock.com/Elena_Danileiko

Page 116 © iStock.com/OlenaMykhaylova

Page 127 © iStock.com/Annalleysh

Page 131 © iStock.com/La_vanda

Page 134 © iStock.com/fabiodinatale

Page 139 © iStock.com/Victority

Page 145 © iStock.com/bhofack2

Page 147 © iStock.com/Kapstun

Page 151 © iStock.com/leekris

Page 152 © iStock.com/Bojsha65

Page 155 © iStock.com/alexandrumagurean

Page 157 © iStock.com/YelenaYemchuk

Page 161 © iStock.com/TVAllen_CDI

Page 165 © iStock.com/tsvibrav

Page 168 © iStock.com/dannikonov

Page 172 © iStock.com/nata_zhekova

Page 176 © iStock.com/YuriyS

Page 178 © iStock.com/PierreDesrosiers

Page 180 © iStock.com/peangdao

Page 184 © iStock.com/arhendrix

Page 187 © iStock.com/voraorn

Page 189 © iStock.com/Maya23K

Page 194 © iStock.com/natenn

Page 197 © iStock.com/circlePS

Page 203 © iStock.com/DronG

Page 209 © iStock.com/Floortje

Page 215 © iStock.com/StephanieFrey

INDEX

ackee, 92

Anadama Bread, 210

Angels on Horseback, 12

anglerfish, 77

aphrodisiac, 5

apples, 152

    Apple & Caramel Bread Pudding, 218

    Apple Dumplings, 154

    Apple Snow, 156

    Arugula Salad with Sliced Apples, Shaved
        Beets, Toasted Walnuts, and Goat
        Cheese, 156

    Baked Onion Apple Cider Soup with
        Smoked Cheddar Cheese Gratiné, 159

    Broiled Butternut Squash with Apples, 190

    Calville Blanc d'Hiver apples, 155

    Cider, 157, 158, 159, 160, 190

    molasses, 157, 160

    Scott Farm's Tarte Tatin, 155

Apple Cider, 157, 158, 159, 160, 190

Apple Cider Molasses, 160

Apple Cider Vinaigrette, 158

apple cider vinegar, 194

artichoke hearts, 33, 48

asparagus, 62

avocado, 8, 61, 67

Avocado-Lime Mayonnaise, 61

bacon, 12, 13, 23, 26, 27, 63, 83, 86, 89,
      105, 128, 130, 186, 201, 205

Baked Cod with Shallots and Lemon, 90

Baked Haddock with Crumb Topping, 106

Baked Onion Apple Cider Soup with Smoked
    Cheddar Cheese Gratiné, 159

Baked Striped Bass with Bacon, 83

banana, 171

Barbecued Shrimp Skewers, 73

Basic Boiled Lobster, 57

Basic Boiled or Steamed Blue Crabs, 47

Basic Steamed Clams, 21

bass, 79

    Baked Striped Bass with Bacon, 83

    Salt-Crusted Black Sea Bass, 81

    Striped Bass with Julienned Vegetables and
        Red Pepper Coulis, 82

bay scallops, 35. *See also* scallops.

Bay Seasoning, 12, 52, 71, 104

beans, 180

    Baked Beans, 181

    cranberry beans, 185

    Jacob's Cattle Bean Stew with Fennel and
        Swiss Chard, 182

    lima beans, 185

    Pickled Green Beans, 196

    Roasted Pumpkin and Bean Spread, 191

beef brisket, 207

beef stew meat, 205

beets, 156, 206, 207

bisque, 42, 71, 188. *See also* chowders.

Bisquick mix, 177

bittersweet chocolate, 175

bivalves, 35

Blackened Swordfish, 144

Blethen, Brandon, 219

Bloody Mary, 3, 8

blueberries, 161

    Blueberry Balsamic Glaze, 164

    Blueberry Grunt, 162

    Ellie's Famous Blueberry Cake, 163

    Peach and Blueberry Crisp, 174

Blueberry Balsamic Glaze, 164

Blueberry Grunt, 162

bluefish, 80
blue mussels. *See* mussels.
bluepoints. *See* oysters.
Boiled Lobster, 57
Boquerones (Portuguese-Style Smelts), 133
Bouillabaisse, 50
Bread and Baked Goods, 209
    Anadama Bread, 210
    Apple & Caramel Bread Pudding, 218
    Corn Bread, 211
    Parker House Rolls, 212
    Pumpkin Whoopie Pies, 220
    Steamed Brown Bread, 214
Bread and Butter Pickles, 194
Broiled Butternut Squash with Apples, 190
Broiled Mussels with Parsley-Artichoke
    Pesto, 33
Broiled Shad Roe, 129
Brown Sage Butter, 100
Brussels sprouts, 179
butternut squash, 190, 192
Butternut Squash Custard, 192
butters
    Brown Sage Butter, 100
    Peach Butter, 173
    Maître d'Hotel Butter, 129

cabbage, 208
Cajun Shrimp Sauté, 70
calamari, 136, 137
    Calamari Fritti, 137
    Calamari Trizzano, 136
California Roll Oysters, 6, 8
candlefish, 131. *See also* smelts.
Cape Cod Cranberry Growers
    Association, 168
capers, 96, 116
carrots, 122, 180, 188, 205
casseroles
    New England Lobster Casserole, 59

cataplana dishes, 69
caviar, 101, 125, 126
ceviche, 41, 109
Chanterelle and Corn Bisque, 188
cheese
    cheddar, 159
    goat, 44, 156
    gruyere, 159
    swiss, 159
cherries
    Cherry and Plum Slump, 166
    Rum Cherries, 166
Cherry and Plum Slump, 166
cherrystones, 15, 19, 21, 22, 23.
    See also clams.
Chili-Lime Mayonnaise, 93
Chilled Northern Shrimp Salad in
    Avocado, 67
chowders, 11. *See also* bisque.
    Corn Chowder, 186
    Fish Chowder, 86
    Flo's Rhode Island Clam Chowder, 27
    Manhattan Clam Chowder, 25
    Nantucket Scallop Chowder, 42
    New England Clam Chowder, 26
    Smoky Haddock Chowder, 105
citrus, 41, 109, 115, 121
clambakes, 14, 15, 16–19
clam chowder, 25, 27
clams, 14
    Basic Steamed Clams, 21
    Clams Casino, 23
    Flo's Rhode Island Clam Chowder, 27
    Grilled Littleneck Clams with Garlic and
        Parsley, 22
    harvesting, 15
    Manhattan Clam Chowder, 25
    New England Clam Chowder, 26
    Shrimp and Clams *Cataplana*, 69
    Spaghetti with White Clam Sauce, 24

steamers, 16

types of, 15

Clams Casino, 23

Clarkdale Farm, 154

Cocktail Sauce, 7

coconut, 32, 64

cod, 84

    Baked Cod with Shallots and Lemon, 90

    Salt Cod Cakes with Chili-Lime
        Mayonnaise, 93

    family, 84

    Fish Chowder, 86

    Jamaican Salt Cod, 92

    Kedgeree, 87

    Oven-Roasted Cod with Lobster, Corn,
        Potato, and Cream, 89

    Roast Cod with Potato-Horseradish
        Crust, 88

    salted, 90

Cod Cakes with Chili-Lime Mayonnaise, 93

coquilles Saint-Jacques, 35

corn

    Chanterelle and Corn Bisque, 188

    Corn Bread, 211

    Corn Chowder, 186

    New England Succotash, 185

    succotash, 185

Corned Beef, 207

Corned Beef Hash, 208

cornmeal, 211, 214

coulis

    Red Pepper Coulis, 82

    Sun-Dried Tomato Coulis, 110

Coville, Frederick, 161

crab, 45

    Basic Boiled or Steamed Blue Crabs, 47

    Crab and Artichoke Dip, 48

    Crab Boil, 47

    Crab Cakes, 49

    Crab Cioppino, 50

Crab Louis, 48

Crab-Stuffed Flounder Roulades, 98

    eating, 45–46

    Individual Maine Crabmeat
        Soufflés, 51

    Pan-Fried Soft-Shell Crab, 52

    types of, 45

Crab and Artichoke Dip, 48

Crab Cakes, 49

Crab Cioppino, 50

Crab Louis, 48

Crab-Stuffed Flounder Roulades, 98

cranberries

    Cranberry, Banana, and White
        Chocolate Muffins, 171

    dried cranberries, 169

    Uncle's Spiced Cranberry Jelly, 170

    Wild Rice-Cranberry Soup, 169

Cranberry, Banana, and White
    Chocolate Muffins, 171

cream cheese, 68, 126, 220

crème fraîche, 127

crustaceans, 45

cucumbers (pickling), 194

cusk, 84, 85, 102

cuttlefish, 134

dips

    Crab and Artichoke Dip, 48

doormats, 95

dry sherry, 169, 188

duck

    fat, 199

    giblets, 199

    duckling, 198

Ducktrap River Fish Farms, 114

Durgin Park, 181

Easy Strawberry Shortcake, 177

Ellie's Famous Blueberry Cake, 163

endive, 146, 199
Escalloped Scallops, 40

Fancy Roast Oysters, 9
Farmer, Fannie, 28, 156, 170
fennel, 115, 119, 166, 182
fin fish, 74, 134. *See also* specific fish,
　　e.g., bass.
　　choosing fresh fish, 76
　　curing, 120, 121
　　smoked, 120
finnan haddie, 84, 101, 105
Fish-and-Chips, 103
Fish Chowder, 86
fishing boats, 75, 141
fishing industry, 4, 116, 117
flatfish, 94
Flo's Rhode Island Clam Chowder, 27
flounder, 94
　　Crab-Stuffed Flounder Roulades, 98
　　Flounder Bonne Femme, 99
　　Flounder Pie, 98
　　Pan-Fried Flounder with Brown
　　　Sage Butter, 100
　　types of, 94–95
Flounder Bonne Femme, 99
Flounder Pie, 98
fluke, 96. *See also* flounder.
fowl
　　Grilled Quail, 200
　　Honey-Glazed Duck, 198
　　Jacques Pepin's Duck Giblet Salad, 199
　　Roast Goose with Sherry-Orange
　　　Glaze, 201
　　Roasted Heritage Turkey, 202
Fried Parsnip Fritters, 193
Fried Smelts, 132
frittata
　　Smoked Salmon Frittata, 123
Fruit, 152–77

Glazed Root Vegetables, 179
goat cheese, 44, 156
Goodband, Zeke, 155
Goodwin, Ali, 177
goose, 180, 201
Gravlax, 121
green beans, 148, 196
Green Bean Salad, 148
gremolata, 143
Grilled Halibut with Nectarine-Poblano
　　Salsa, 111
Grilled Littleneck Clams with Garlic and
　　Parsley, 22
Grilled Lobster-tails with Avocado-Lime
　　Mayonnaise, 61
Grilled Mackerel with Citrus and
　　Fennel, 115
Grilled Peaches with Molten Chocolate, 175
Grilled Quail, 200
Grilled Swordfish with Mint Gremolata, 143

haddock, 101
　　Baked Haddock with Crumb
　　　Topping, 106
　　Oven-"Fried" Fish-and-Chips, 103
　　Smoky Haddock Chowder, 105
hake, 84–85
Hale, Sara Josepha, 113, 177
halibut, 107
　　Grilled Halibut with Nectarine-
　　　Poblano Salsa, 111
　　Oil-Poached Halibut with Sun-Dried
　　　Tomato Coulis, 110
heirloom apples, 153, 154, 155
herring, 113, 126
Honey-Glazed Duck, 198
horseradish, 7, 11, 37, 88, 142
Hunter's Pie, 205

Individual Maine Crabmeat Soufflés, 51

Jasper White's Pan-Roasted Whole Flounder or Fluke with Brown Butter, Lemon, and Capers, 96
Jacques Pepin's Duck Giblet Salad, 199
Jamaican Salt Cod, 92
Johnny Cake, 211
Jones, Judith, 199

K Farm, 172
Kedgeree, 84, 87
King Arthur Flour, 171, 216

leek, 69, 72, 122, 123, 188
legumes, 178. *See also* beans.
lemon sole, 94. *See also* flounder.
Lincoln, Mary Johnson Bailey, 193
littlenecks, 15, 21, 22, 24, 26, 69. *See also* clams.
lobster, 53
    Basic Boiled Lobster, 53, 57
    bisque, 53
    buying, 55
    fishing, 54
    Grilled Lobster-tails with Avocado-Lime Mayonnaise, 61
    harvesting, 54
    how to eat, 55
    Lobster and Asparagus Risotto with Truffle Oil, 62
    Lobster Croquettes, 60
    Lobster Mac 'n' Cheese, 63
    Lobster Rolls, 53, 58
    New England Lobster Casserole, 59
    Oven-Roasted Cod with Lobster, Corn, Potato, and Cream, 89
    salad, 57
    steaming, 57
    terms, 55
Lobster and Asparagus Risotto with Truffle Oil, 62

Lobster Croquettes, 60
Lobster Rolls, 53

mackerel, 112
    Grilled Mackerel with Citrus and Fennel, 115
    Smoked Mackerel Pâté, 114
Maine Organic Farmers and Growers Association, 181
Maître d'Hotel Butter, 129
Mallet, Evan, 188
Manhattan Clam Chowder, 25
maple syrup, 216
Maple Walnut Pie, 216
marinade, 41, 138, 200
Marinated Grilled Squid Salad, 138
mayonnaise
    Avocado-Lime Mayonnaise, 61
    Chili-Lime Mayonnaise, 93
meat and game
    Corned Beef, 207
    Corned Beef Hash, 208
    Hunter's Pie, 205
    Slow-Braised Pork Roast with Roasted Root Vegetables, 206
    Venison Meatloaf, 204
mercury, 70, 77
Mignonette Sauce, 7
Mint Gremolata, 143
Miso-Soy Glazed Salmon, 119
Mitchell, Paulette, 169
molasses, 157, 175, 181, 191
mushrooms, 40, 59, 72, 83, 99, 123, 188, 205
mussels, 28, 32
    Broiled Mussels with Parsley-Artichoke Pesto, 33
    harvesting, 29
    Mussels Fra Diavolo, 31
    Mussels Steamed in White Wine, 30

preparing for cooking, 29
Spicy Thai Mussels, 32
types of, 29
Mussels Fra Diavolo, 31
Mussels Steamed in White Wine, 30
Mustard-Herb Crust, 142

Nantucket Scallop Chowder, 42
Nectarine-Poblano Salsa, 111
New England Boiled Dinner, 207
New England Clam Chowder, 26
New England Lobster Casserole, 59
New England Succotash, 185
New Potatoes with Caviar and Crème
 Fraîche, 125
Northern beans, 191

Oil-Poached Halibut with Sun-Dried
 Tomato Coulis, 110
Oven-"Fried" Fish-and-Chips, 103
Oven-Roasted Cod with Lobster, Corn,
 Potato, and Cream, 89
Oyster Stew, 10
oysters, 2
 Angels on Horseback, 12
 aphrodisiac, 5
 "California Roll" oysters, 8
 Fancy Roast Oysters, 9
 on the half shell, 6
 harvesting, 4
 opening, 6
 Oyster Stew, 10
 Oysters Rockefeller, 13
 types of, 5
Oysters Rockefeller, 13

Pan-Fried Flounder with Brown Sage
 Butter, 100
Pan-Fried Soft-Shell Crab, 52

Pan-Roasted Swordfish with Mustard-Herb
 Crust, 142
Parker House Rolls, 212
Parloa, Maria, 156
Parsley-Artichoke Pesto, 33
pasta, 23, 24, 31, 33, 72, 100, 136
pâté, 114
Peach and Blueberry Crisp, 174
peaches, 172
 Grilled Peaches with Molten
  Chocolate, 174
 Peach and Blueberry Crisp, 174
 Peach Butter, 173
peas, 122
Pepin, Jacques, 199
pesto, 33
 Parsley-Artichoke Pesto, 33
pickles
 Bread and Butter Pickles, 194
poaching, 110
poblano chile, 41, 111
pollock, 85, 126
pork loin, 206
potatoes, 3, 19, 24, 25, 26, 27, 42, 64, 86,
 88, 93, 103, 105, 125, 186, 208
Potted Shrimp, 68
prawns. See shrimp.
preserves
 Pickled Green Beans, 196
pumpkins
 Pumpkin Indian Pudding, 219
 Pumpkin Whoopie Pies, 220
 Roasted Pumpkin and Bean
  Spread, 191

quail, 200
quahogs, 15, 23, 27, 29.
 See also clams.

rabbits, 205

Red Pepper Coulis, 82
Red Tide, 16
restaurants
    1794 Watchtide by the Sea, 51
    Black Trumpet, 188
    Durgin Park, 181
    Fore Street, 148
    La Moia Tapas Bar & Cafe, 133
    Lindbergh's Crossing, 188
    Parker House, 212
    Robert's Maine Grill, 89
    Union Oyster House, 11, 211
Rhode Island Clam Chowder, 27
risotto
    Lobster and Asparagus Risotto, 62
Roast Cod with Potato-Horseradish
        Crust, 88
Roast Goose with Sherry-Orange
        Glaze, 201
Roasted Garlic and Yellow Pepper Sauce, 43
Roasted Heritage Turkey, 202
Roasted Pumpkin and Bean Spread, 191
rockweed, 18–19
roe, 8, 35, 96, 124, 126, 129, 130
rolled oats, 174
rum, 166
Rum Cherries, 166
rutabaga, 179

Sacred Cod, 124
salads
    Arugula Salad with Sliced Apples, Shaved
        Beets, Toasted Walnuts, and Goat
        Cheese, 156
    Chilled Northern Shrimp Salad in
        Avocado, 67
    Green Bean Salad, 148
    Jacques Pepin's Duck Giblet
        Salad, 199
    Marinated Grilled Squid Salad, 138

salmon,
    Gravlax, 121
    Miso-Soy Glazed Salmon, 119
    Salmon and Leek Pie, 122
    Salmon with Tri-Pepper Salsa, 118
    Smoked Salmon Frittata, 123
    smoking, 120
Salmon with Tri-Pepper Salsa, 119
salsa
    Nectarine-Poblano Salsa, 111
    Tri-Pepper Salsa, 118
salt cod, 90, 93
Salt-Crusted Black Sea Bass, 81
salt pork, 86, 105, 181, 185
Sam Hayward's Tuna and Green Bean
        Salad, 148
sauces
    Cocktail Sauce, 7, 20
    Mignonette Sauce, 7, 20
    Roasted Garlic and Yellow Pepper
        Sauce, 43
    Tartar Sauce, 49, 95, 104, 132
    White Clam Sauce, 24
    White Sauce, 40, 60
Sautéed Shad Roe with Applewood
        Bacon, 130
scallops, 34
    Broiled Scallops with Prosciutto, 37
    Crispy Oven "Fried" Scallops, 36
    Dave K's Scallop Casserole, 38
    Escalloped Scallops, 40
    harvesting, 34, 35
    Nantucket Scallop Chowder, 42
    Seared Scallops with Roasted Garlic
        and Yellow Pepper Sauce, 43
    types of, 35
Scott Farms Orchard, 155
Scott Farm's Tarte Tatin, 155
scrod, 84, 85
sea scallops. *See* scallops.

Seared Scallops with Roasted Garlic
and Yellow Pepper Sauce, 43
Seared Sea Scallops on Wilted
Greens, 44
Seared Tuna in a Black and White
Sesame Crust, 147
sesame, 73, 147
shad and shad roe, 124
Broiled Shad Roe, 129
Connecticut Stuffed Baked Shad, 128
New Potatoes with Caviar and
Crème Fraîche, 127
Sautéed Shad Roe with Applewood
Bacon, 130
shallots, 90
shrimp, 64
Barbecued Shrimp Skewers, 73
Cajun Shrimp Sauté, 70
Chilled Northern Shrimp Salad in
Avocado, 67
how to peel and devein, 67
Potted Shrimp, 68
Shrimp and Clams *Cataplana*, 69
types of, 64, 66
Wild Mushroom and Shrimp
Linguine, 72
Shrimp and Clams *Cataplana*, 69
Slow-Braised Pork Roast with Roasted
Root Vegetables, 206
smelts, 131
Boquerones (Portuguese-Style
Smelts), 133
Fried Smelts, 132
Smoked Mackerel Pâté, 114
smoked salmon, 116
Smoked Salmon Frittata, 123
Smoky Haddock Chowder, 105
sole
Flounder Bonne Femme, 99
soufflé, 51

squash, 189
Broiled Butternut Squash with
Apples, 190
Butternut Squash Custard, 192
Spaghetti with White Clam Sauce, 24
Spicy Thai Mussels, 32
spinach, 13, 44
squid, 134
Calamari Fritti, 137
Calamari Trizzano, 136
Marinated Grilled Squid Salad, 138
Steamed Blue Crabs, 47
Steamed Brown Bread, 214
Steamed Clams, 21
steamers, 16, 21. *See also* clams.
stews
Bouillabaisse, 50
Crab Cioppino, 50
Jacob's Cattle Bean Stew with Fennel
and Swiss Chard, 182
Oyster Stew, 10
stock
beef, 159
Strawbery (*sic*) Banke, 176
strawberries
Easy Strawberry Shortcake, 177
ice cream, 177
Striped Bass with Julienned Vegetables
and Red Pepper Coulis, 82
succotash 185. *See also* corn.
Sun-Dried Tomato Coulis, 82
sushi, 113, 147
swiss chard, 182
swordfish, 139
Blackened Swordfish, 144
Grilled Swordfish with Mint
Gremolata, 143
Pan-Roasted Swordfish with
Mustard-Herb Crust, 142

tarragon, 81, 83, 121
Tartar Sauce, 49, 95, 104, 132
Thai Mussels, 32
tomalley, 55, 56
tomcod, 85, 101
Tri-Pepper Salsa, 118
truffle oil, 62
tuna, 126, 145
  Sam Hayward's Tuna and Green
    Bean Salad, 148
  Seared Tuna in a Black and White
    Sesame Crust, 147
  Tuna Tartare in Endive Boats, 146
Tuna Tartare in Endive Boats, 146
turbot, 107
turkey, 191, 202

Uncle's Spiced Cranberry Jelly, 170
Union Oyster House, 10, 11, 181, 211

vegetables
  Glazed Root Vegetables, 179
  Slow-Braised Pork Roast with Roasted
    Root Vegetables, 206

Venison Meatloaf, 204
vermouth, red, 164
vermouth, white, 31, 42, 68

walnuts, 156, 171, 216
Wampanoag, 168, 204
wheat germ, 174
white chocolate, 171
White Clam Sauce, 24
White, Elizabeth, 161
white fish, 84
White, Jasper, 96, 186
White Pea beans, 181
White Sauce, 40, 60
Wild Mushroom and Shrimp
    Linguine, 72
Wild Rice-Cranberry Soup, 169
wine, 18, 21, 24, 30, 186, 206
Wyman's, 163

Yellow Eye beans, 181

ABOUT THE AUTHOR

Currently Contributing Editor to The Cook's Cook digital magazine, **Jean Kerr** was the co-founder and former Editor-in-Chief of *Northeast FLAVOR* magazine, the first New England regional food and wine magazine. *FLAVOR* was named one of the Top 10 new magazines in the U.S. after its first year of publication by Media Source/Kirkus Reviews. She is also a food writer, chef, and author of three cookbooks to date: *Mystic Seafood, The Union Oyster House Cookbook*, and *Windjammer Cooking*. She is a two-time Book of the Year Award nominee.

Jean has traveled widely, throughout the U.S. and beyond, as a ship's cook, doing cooking demos, and has been a frequent guest on both television and radio shows. She is a sought-after judge of culinary competitions, and a frequent emcee at food events. She is a member of the prestigious invitation-only society Les Dames d'Escoffier.

More praise for *The Mystic Cookbook*

"Here are great seafood recipes, anecdotes about fish and fishing, and the history of New England seafood. Entertaining and informative reading."

—Linda Greenlaw, author of *The Hungry Ocean, The Lobster Chronicles, Recipes from a Very Small Island*, and more New England favorites

"Get out your lobster pot, your clam and oyster knives, and a big appetite. . . . Jean Kerr's description of a traditional New England clam bake, odd tidbits about oysters, lobsters, and scallops will have you shaking your head: 'Hey, I didn't know that!' This is a terrific addition to the legions of great cookbooks devoted to the subject of New England seafood!"

—Kathy Gunst, Cordon Bleu trained chef, James Beard Award for Home Cooking winner, cookbook author, food writer, and former culinary editor of *Food and Wine* magazine

"Jean Kerr has a wonderful sense of food, particularly from a historic viewpoint, with her knowledge of the old and tried combinations that have made New England and Mystic Seaport great places to sit down and have a simply made but delicious soup, casserole, or baked, fried, steamed, or grilled piece of fish."

—Master Chef James Haller, author of five cookbooks, including *The Blue Strawberry Cookbook* and *Cooking in the Shaker Spirit*